FROM HERE
TO HERE
STORIES INSPIRED BY LONDON'S CIRCLE LINE

Edited by John Simmons, Neil Taylor,
Tim Rich and Tom Lynham
Photographs by Jessie Simmons

CYANBOOKS

This book was written before the tragic events of 7 July 2005 when London was attacked by terrorists. This note has been added as the book was going to press. From Here to Here *was written as a celebration of a diverse, cosmopolitan city, a city of all races, languages and faiths. We are proud of London and saddened by the indiscriminate actions of terrorists. If parts of this book seem at all insensitive in the light of those events, we apologise.*

We dedicate this book to London and the victims of the 7 July attacks.

Text copyright © 2005 Simon Armitage,
Jayne Workman, Mike Reed, Elise Valmorbida,
Tom Lynham, Rishi Dastidar, Karen McCarthy,
Anelia Schutte, Tim Segaller, Neil Taylor,
Dan Germain, Simon Jones, Nick Asbury,
Tim Rich, Rob Williams, Tim Coates, David May,
Dan Radley, Will Awdry, Martin Gorst,
Gordon Kerr, Sarah McCartney, Lisa Desforges,
Laura Forman, Ian Marchant, David Varela,
Steve Mullins, Stuart Delves, Richard Owsley,
Jim Davies, John Simmons

Photographs copyright © 2005 Jessie Simmons

First published in Great Britain in 2005 by
Cyan Books, an imprint of

Cyan Communications Limited
4.3 The Ziggurat
60–66 Saffron Hill
London EC I N 8QX
United Kingdom
www.cyanbooks.com

A CIP record for this book is available from the
British Library

ISBN I-904879-35-7

Book design by R&D&Co

Printed and bound in Great Britain by
TJ International, Padstow, Cornwall

CONTENTS

PREFACE

This collection of writing was inspired by London Underground's Circle Line. There is something inherently right about the association of circles and storytelling. "Gather round." We get together in circles to tell and listen to stories. And there is always a satisfaction in a circular narrative that brings you back at the end to the place where you started. Particularly as the journey enables you to see that place differently because of the experiences along the way.

The storytelling mode of *From here to here* might be called circular–linear. It starts and ends at King's Cross, travelling around the Circle Line. It starts with poetry and foreboding about the present and the future; it ends with prose and elegiac memories of the past; and it stops at genres and emotions in between. Perhaps the most universal of metaphors applied to life is that of the journey. We invite you onto this journey by Tube, stopping at each station on the Circle Line to explore the character of each place through fact and fiction, poetry and prose, pathos and humour. In doing so you will experience the diversity of London itself – its history, its present and its future, its range of characters and places – through a variety of literary styles that will keep you intrigued and entertained.

Some of the 31 writers here will be well-known to readers. Simon Armitage, for example, is generally considered the leading poet of his generation. But many of the writers are not widely known except in the world of writing for business. You might well have read their words before but not realised it – for example on a label for Innocent smoothies (Dan Germain), on packaging for Lush soap (Sarah McCartney), or on a Penguin poster (Rob Williams). Most of the writers here write every day for the companies, brands and organisations that are the backdrops to our lives. They write the words that go into brochures, annual reports, point of sale, packaging, press releases, articles, advertising, training manuals. Words are our everyday currency and the people involved in this book spend their lives professionally tendering words. But they are passionate about words, they value them and love using them, and they want others to share their enjoyment.

The writers are all members of 26, a not-for-profit association set up to champion the cause of better writing at work and in life. *From here to here* started out as a collaboration between 26, London Underground, particularly its Platform for Art programme, and the staff and students of the London College of Communications. Outcomes of that collaboration, part of the London Design Festival 2005, included an exhibition and a series of posters on Circle Line trains and stations.

This book is the elder child of that partnership. The writers were each assigned a subject – one of the 27 stations on the Circle Line, plus a "lost" station, the Control Room and the river. The brief was open, but with a 2,500-word limit. London Underground staff volunteered to help with information and behind-the-scenes tours. The writers were invited to respond in the way they felt most appropriate. As a result we received short stories, poems, Arabian Nights tales, memoirs, fables, guided tours, reportage, comic essays, historical documents, autobiographical remembrances: words to make you pause and look around at your surroundings with fresh eyes, words to make you observe, imagine, wonder, think and sometimes laugh out loud. Who would have thought, for example, that Euston Square held such hilarious secrets? Then again, perhaps it never has, except in the imagination of a writer.

That is the real joy of *From here to here*. It shows that writing can deepen your understanding of a place through a better understanding of our shared humanity. In doing so it reaches out to everyone who ever visits, lives or works in London – or who might one day do any of those things. It will tell you more about the reality of this great city than any conventional travel guide. It is an alternative, sometimes an antidote, sometimes a companion, to such guides. It will take you to places, not least in your imagination, that other guides never reach. You have a journey before you, made up of many stories. London itself is a never-ending story, a city of constant discovery. We ask you to see it through the eyes of 31 writers, and we believe you will be richer for the experience.

John Simmons

KING'S CROSS

KX

Simon Armitage

Northerner, this is your stop. This longhouse
of echoing echoes and sooted glass,
this goth pigeon hangar, this diesel roost
is the end of the line. Brace and be brisk,
commoner, carry your heart like an egg
on a spoon, be fleet through the concourse, primed
for that point in time when the world goes bust,
when the unattended holdall or case
unloads its cache of fanaticised heat.

Here's you after the fact, found by torchlight,
being-less, heaped, boned of all thought and sense.
The camera can barely look. Or maybe,
just maybe, you live. Here's you on the News,
shirtless, minus a limb, exiting smoke
to a backdrop of red melt, onto streets
paved with gilt, begging a junkie for help.

Tales of the river

Jayne Workman

From country stream to medieval gutter; from twelfth-century spa to eighteenth-century sewer; from river of death to saviour of life – the Fleet River has made its mark on Farringdon. Or rather Farringdon has made its mark on the Fleet River. For today, all traces of the once-powerful waterway have been erased, its identity denied, buried, forgotten.

But what was this identity and what secrets lie hidden behind the modern concrete and corporate name-plaques? Go back just two or three centuries and the landscape was very different, one where the Fleet not only existed but dominated the lives lived on its banks. Indeed, such was the influence of the river that many of the buildings and thoroughfares along its course took its name in deference. Fleet Prison, Fleet Street, Fleet Bridge, Fleet Market, Fleet Weddings, Fleet Valley, Fleet Ditch and the Fleet Rules were all children born of the dark coupling of the river with the people of the city. And this is its story, the story of the invisible Fleet and modern-day Farringdon: a story of power, loss and redemption.

The story opens in the spa village of Hampstead – Caen Wood to be exact, now Kenwood – where the Fleet had its source. From these innocent origins, the river meandered south, drawn by gravity through what is now Kentish Town, St Pancras, Clerkenwell and Farringdon, before meeting the Thames by Blackfriars Bridge four miles later. But something happened along the way. By the time it reached the City, the Fleet had assumed a different character. In fact, it was barely a river at all. Tired and dirty from the journey, its village spring waters had become a putrid sludge of sewage, animal carcasses, offal and mud, the shame of London.

But it hadn't always been that way. The transformation took place gradually, over time as well as distance. Back in the twelfth century, the Fleet's banks were dotted with wells said to have healing qualities. By the thirteenth century, it flowed freely enough for light shipping, and pollution set in. By the sixteenth century, it was shallow and slow-running, clogged and stinking with dirt and debris.

During the Restoration and into the eighteenth century, the Fleet was at its ugliest and most notorious. Despite many attempts to civilise it, the river became more and more unruly. It was a dumping ground not just for raw sewage and rubbish, but for bodies too, the victims of murderous thieves or their own drunken carelessness. Animal carcasses and bloody waste from Smithfield market a few yards upstream were tossed into the Fleet alongside human corpses. It was a river of death in other ways too: the toxic water, the nauseating fumes – people died just from being close to it. Both the Great Plague of 1664–65 and the city's cholera outbreaks were blamed on the Fleet's rat-infested waters.

Notoriety, rather than dampening the river's appetite, fuelled its ambition, its diminished waters no barrier to expansion. In fact, the more constricted and congested the river grew, the more invasive it became. Every wave of dank air that rose from its sludge was a clammy hand laid on the city's landmarks, each one taking its oppressor's name. The Fleet's empire grew.

What was life in this empire like? Let's take the Fleet Rules, the lawless margin between the most westerly walls of the City of London (today's Aldersgate and Newgate Street) and the Liberties, the outer jurisdiction of the City government (roughly Temple Bar on Fleet Street). In this, one of London's most desperate neighbourhoods, the Fleet ruled, the dark heart at its centre. Within its shroud, evil thrived; the area became a haven for murderers, prostitutes and thieves, its small courtyards and alleyways of ill-kept, grubby houses, steeped in the river's mist, cover for a life of concealment. But no matter how squalid or unfashionable, the warren of grimy streets still teemed with people, all strangely drawn by the river's unhealthy atmosphere.

The Fleet was aided in its quest for power by another Fleet phenomenon: Fleet weddings, clandestine marriages carried out within the Fleet Rules. The lawlessness that drew the city's criminals also permitted couples the earliest quickie weddings. Seduced by the promise of speed and secrecy at little cost, they flocked to the area in their thousands, their ebb and flow echoing that of the Fleet itself. It was within the damp walls of the Fleet Prison chapel that the first of these weddings took place. The prison, located on the eastern banks of the Fleet, today's Farringdon Street, was Fleet property through and through. Steeped in the river's malodorous vapours, said to have even killed prisoners, it was the most unlikely of wedding venues. And the weddings themselves were not immune to its contagion. Rumours of dark motives were rife: heiresses kidnapped and married for their fortunes, bigamy, illegitimacy and rape all loomed large in the unscrupulous trade.

Money did too. And many stood to profit. Not least the river itself, its reputation bolstered by the flood of new visitors to its banks. Never more so than when the Fleet weddings burst out of the grim confines of the prison and into the Rules. Marriage-houses quickly sprang up in its shops, taverns and coffeehouses, residents quick to capitalise on a new opportunity for money making, the river their silent witness.

To the west of the prison was Fleet Market, another Fleet outpost. Built in the 1730s on the newly bricked-over stretch of the river, it was a short whiff upstream of the still-open sewer of the Fleet leading south to the Thames. In fact, the fumes would accompany the sale of its fruit, vegetables and meat for the best part of a century. Like the other Fleet offspring, the market attracted its own refugees from the city's margins. Drawn by the promise of food scraps and casual labour as porters or basket women, the homeless and disreputable slept under the market's cover or squatted in the abandoned and half-finished houses nearby. Many were found lying about with no good account of themselves, or discovered in garrets, starving or on the brink of death. For a hundred years until the market was demolished, fights, pickpocketing, stabbings and prostitution were as much a feature of market life as the stalls themselves, adding to the Fleet's reputation for lawlessness and depravity.

Just a short distance upstream, you might hear, carried on the river's breath, the lowing, squealing and bleating of cows, pigs and sheep, all waiting their turn in the steaming pens of nearby Smithfield market. Animals had been killed here for nearly a thousand years, the bloody trade making its own contribution to the Fleet's aura of death. Leading to Smithfield from the river were Turnmill and Cowcross Street, by today's Farringdon station. Animals were herded through these streets, along the Fleet, over low bridges, to their slaughter under the butcher's blade. Here, where frightened animals rampaged, trampling victims under foot, street-sellers hawked everything from Hammersmith strawberries to Covent Garden violets, stay-laces to stationery. On one corner an oyster seller; on the next a watercress girl. Mixed with the sellers' cries were those of the animals as they smelt on the Fleet their own violent end.

So when did it all change? And how? The Fleet, it seemed, was invincible, its influence never greater, its empire never stronger. But it was at this zenith that the tipping-point came: the point when power turned to loss and the empire crumbled. Today, the only vestige of the Fleet is Fleet Street, one last nod towards the wayward river. But even here life has drained away. The newspaper presses thunder in Fleet Street no longer, but in Wapping. In Farringdon, where it left its deepest mark, the Fleet was usurped.

It started in 1732 with a brutal measure: the bricking-over of the Fleet from Fleet Street to Holborn Bridge. This act signalled the

beginning of the end of the river's reign, an unceremonious dethrone-
ment that took more than a century to achieve as each finger of the
river's stranglehold was slowly prised free. The shame that the Fleet
had for so long visited upon the capital was now its own.

Once the Fleet was bricked over, the way was clear to build.
In 1738, when a street was built over the old river, it was to
William Farendon, not the Fleet, that the city turned for a name
to bestow on the new construction. A merchant of the Gold-
smiths Company, Farendon had purchased the local ward in
1279, becoming its alderman two years later. Farendon became
Farringdon, and Farringdon Street was born.

With the creation of Farringdon Street, the river began to lose
its grip over the area it had dominated for so long. For it was
Farringdon Street that gave its name to the terminal of London's
first underground railway line that opened here 125 years later,
changing not just the name but the character of the area for good.

Further indignities were quick to follow. In 1754, Fleet weddings
were outlawed; then in 1763 came the bricking-over of the second
stretch of the Fleet, from Fleet Street to the Thames. By the turn
of the century, every last inch of the river in the city had been
hidden from view. And with the subversion of the Fleet River
went the Fleet empire, its fall from power complete with the
demolition in 1826 of Fleet Market and in 1846 of Fleet Prison.

Or in name, at least.

Just a decade or so later, when plans for London's first underground railway were mooted, it was to the Fleet that the city's
engineers turned. An 1853 Act had permitted the construction of
a pioneering four-mile line connecting seven stations: Paddington, Edgware Road, Baker Street, Great Portland Street, Euston
Square, King's Cross and Farringdon Street. It was for the final
stage, as the line turned southward towards Farringdon, that the
city looked to the river for direction. The line from King's Cross
to Farringdon Street followed the crease of the Fleet valley.

When work finally started on the line in 1860, the Fleet River
had been bricked over for nearly a hundred years. But for the
many thousands of navvies from all over the country who came
to work on the line, it was still very much a threat to life. And
they were right to fear. The Fleet was responsible for one of the
worst accidents during the construction of this first stretch of
underground railway line.

The Fleet's brick sewer had been weakened in 1862 by the building of the railway, so when a torrential storm hit the capital, it was fit to burst. And burst it did, unleashing the river's toxic waters onto the city again. Scaffolding and beams used to construct the tunnel walls were swept away, and the works disappeared under 10 feet of water. After a two-day battle to contain the floods, a diversion into the Thames was set up, the sewer was rebuilt and the battle with the mighty waterway was won once more.

The Fleet's petulance caused little delay, and within a matter of months, a special train was charted for shareholders and VIPs to showcase the marvels of the golden railway. The official opening was 10 January 1863. Underground travel was an instant success. The people of London were quick to take to this bold concept, with 30,000 passengers on the first day and 11.8 million in the first year. Not a murmur from the Fleet.

There was another important consequence. In 1864, a special worker's fare was introduced, the first ever. Before 6 a.m., you could travel for a fare of just three pence and return on any train. The offer attracted over 300 users a day, then 600 in double-quick time. Over 70 percent of the tickets sold in the early years were third class. This changed the lives of London's workers, and hence London itself. Workers were better off in health and wealth. It was now feasible to live in the cheaper outskirts of the city, in better-quality housing. In time, this provided access to a whole new workforce, fuelling the city's industrial revolution and the population explosion that went with it.

And herein lies the Fleet's redemption, the final chapter of the story. With Farringdon's triumph, paradoxically, came the Fleet's salvation. The advent of the underground railway signalled a new era for its former empire. The worst of its slums cleared, the area once dominated by the Fleet was now identified by its underground station. The shift in power and identity was complete. As for the Fleet itself, the path its currents had carved out more than 2,000 years ago laid the route for a technology that would change the city. We buried the river, then followed it underground. The black river, once a repository and metaphor for the city's ills, had again become a current of life. Today, Farringdon station is London's third busiest, its flow a flow of people, the river, as it always has, exercising its magnetism on the people of the capital.

BARBICAN

All the lonely people

Mike Reed

THIRD DEATH IN "ELEANOR RIGBY" CASE, blared the fat black *Metro* headline. Simon had read the paper earlier. Knew all the details and didn't care for a repeat. Instead, he reminded himself again to buy milk on the way home, and watched a young couple along the carriage coo and giggle at each other. They wore baggy jeans that pooled around their colourful trainers. The American logos on their T-shirts had faded, or been made to look as if they had. The boy nuzzled the girl, making her cackle and swear loudly at him, apparently oblivious to the rest of the passengers.

Next to them, like a sparrow beside a pair of parakeets, a pale, nervous girl sat picking at the thin silver bangle around her wrist. Her tiny hands had long, twig-like fingers and nails bitten raw. Straight, thin hair the colour of milk. She had the look, thought Simon, of a chick that had fallen from its nest: skinny; unparented; lost. He named her Birdgirl.

This was his private game: thinking up names for his fellow passengers. Naming them and imagining histories for them. Constructing a whole community in his head.

Birdgirl had an unconscious tic: a nervous twitch of the head. She flinched and squinted every few minutes, as if some unseen devil was snapping its fingers in her face. It was easy to imagine her alone at a desk on the outskirts of some vast accounts department, pecking dutifully at the keyboard of her PC. Eating her lunch alone, lost in the pages of a fat romantic novel sheathed in library plastic. Then travelling home alone amid the parakeets, the pinstriped starlings, the Soho peacocks. Her song so long drowned out that she simply kept it to herself. Her colours too much like smoke and dust to stand out in the city.

There were so many people like this, he thought. Many more than one might think. They made so little impression, one noticed them only by actively seeking them out. Like the nocturnal animals in a book he remembered from childhood. *How many faces can you find?*

It was the same with the Birdgirls of this world: spectral figures turned almost transparent by silence and isolation. But as with the creatures in the book, once you started seeing them, you saw them everywhere. Like a medium who looks at everyday crowds and sees, streaming through them, the vast innumerable throng of the dead. Those we have forgotten.

Birdgirl looked up suddenly, as if starting from a dream. The train was juddering to a halt. The rush of blurred commuters beyond the window began to resolve into a mass of pale, pinched faces peering in. The train stopped: Farringdon. One more station to go. He watched a knot of passengers form inside the door, then battle through the incoming crowd that was already shoving its frantic way aboard. Empty seats were seized upon. Someone snatched the *Metro* from the seat opposite, sat down and snapped the paper open. He found himself staring at the headline yet again.

THIRD DEATH IN "ELEANOR RIGBY" CASE. WIDOW, 46, "KEPT HERSELF TO HERSELF"

Another Birdgirl. Another of the long-forgotten.

He "lay her down to rest," the paper said, quoting a note found at the scene. The killer had started writing notes after the police described the first murder as "motiveless and brutal." Seemingly disappointed with the reaction, he had felt the need to explain. When they found the second body, the police also discovered a neatly handwritten letter:

She rests at last. Lonely no more. Mercy is the motive, peace the reward. Everyone forgot her but me.

She had been chloroformed unconscious and then smothered. A forensic expert described it as an "almost compassionate" murder, and was immediately forced to apologise for appearing to sympathise with the killer.

The harsh squeal of an electronic alarm announced that the doors were closing. Someone moved along the aisle and blocked Simon's view of the paper. He looked back towards Birdgirl, just visible beyond a shoulder bag that announced itself as *Criminal*. She had stopped picking at the bangle and was reading a crumpled scrap of paper. A shopping list perhaps. A short list. A list for one.

Whatever it was, she folded it now, her spindly fingers pinching it flat, and tucked it into a small pink bag. Her hands knotted themselves back up in her lap.

Simon looked away, scanning the crowd.

Standing against the glass partition was a tall, imposing figure. A man of around 45, Simon guessed, in a long, expensive-looking charcoal overcoat. He leaned against the glass and gripped the top of the pane with a muscular hand. His hair was curly, thick and black. Dark eyebrows shielded piercing pale eyes.

Broad and solid, he stood quite still amid the crowd. *Serene*, thought Simon. A man at peace, unlike poor Birdgirl, twitching at the world. His steady gaze focused somewhere far ahead. Like a captain on his bridge, looking out across the sea.

The Captain. There: he had a name. A fitting name, Simon smiled to himself.

The train was slowing for Barbican. He watched through the trousers and bags as Birdgirl rose uncertainly from her seat. Simon got up too, awkwardly changing places with an anxious-looking woman in a scarlet suit and sharp black spectacles. She flashed him a cold, fast smile.

Shuffling with the others towards the door, he saw not only Birdgirl disembarking but, ahead of her, the Captain too. A party!

Sidling out of the crush, Simon looked along the platform towards the exit. Up ahead he could see the Captain striding confidently away. The other passengers moved almost deferentially around him, giving him room, like tugs around a steamer.

Birdgirl was just a few steps behind, but in a different world. She picked her way gingerly, almost apologetically, and the crowd stepped blindly across her path, jostling her with bags and elbows as if she wasn't there.

Simon glanced up through the open roof of the station. Beyond the bright lights of the platform, two huge serrated silhouettes rose against the sky, windows glowing dully within the concrete. The towers of the Barbican estate.

He trotted up the stairs as the Captain eased his way towards the ticket gates. Birdgirl had stopped and was hunched over her bag, digging at it while people muttered and fussed their way around her. Finally she plucked out a Travelcard, jammed it into a gate and hurried through.

Simon followed, passing his own ticket through the machine as Birdgirl started up the steps towards the street. A trio of tipsy businessmen was coming the other way, and she pressed herself to the wall as they passed, firing off bursts of laughter that cannoned off the tiled walls. As Simon mounted the stairs, Birdgirl was barely ahead of him.

They emerged into the cool November air. Birdgirl hurried towards the street, hugging herself against the breeze. Immediately ahead, the Captain was standing monolithically in front of the *Evening Standard* kiosk. He found some change and handed it over, tucking the late edition under his arm. Simon glimpsed the headline: *TUBE STRIKE THREAT.*

The latest Eleanor Rigby killing had taken less than a day to fall from the headlines. Forgotten once again, the victim slipped back beneath the surface of the city. Imagining her, the unnamed widow, adrift and alone on the ocean of London, Simon felt a stab of sorrow. He tried not to think of her, but his mind insisted on conjuring the image of a simple, well-kept flat; an orderly, sterile life. Early nights to escape the day. Late nights of bright television to ward off the silence. Weeks, months, years – and then a sudden, terrible burst of panic: the fog of chloroform, the awful suffocation.

He shuddered, stepping out onto the concrete bridge that led to the estate. Beneath him, the hot light and clamour of traffic along the Goswell Road. Above him, the empty yellow night. Towering concrete grids the colour of ash, punctuated with pale panels of light. Barbed with jutting balconies like the vertebrae of some great dinosaur.

He crossed the bridge, aware as so often of the vast and seething map that spread itself around him. The rush of lives beyond his knowledge, or even his imagination. Wave upon wave of human beings, caught up in events and conversations he could never know.

The wind butted him like an animal. He hurried off the bridge, feeling the bite of winter in the air, remembering suddenly that he hadn't bought the milk.

"Bugger," he muttered, and paused on the broad, open concourse. He already felt far from the road, shielded within the great fortress of the estate, the traffic no louder than a distant motorway. It was part of the reason he'd chosen this place, pushed his budget to secure the flat.

The centre of the city, he'd thought to himself. Things will change here. I'm at the heart of it all. Things will change.

He dismissed the milk and pressed on, passing into the cool slab of shadow cast by the block to his left. The wind sprang from between the concrete stilts of the raised building, grabbing his coat and shaking it around him. He pulled it tighter, looking up at the deserted walkways running the length of the block. The dim oblongs of front doors. Weak luminescence at windows: the flutter and flash of television sets deep within the concrete.

He'd been thrilled at the idea of living so close to the theatre, the gallery, the cinema. He made lists of what to see and ticked them off. He had four years of programmes on the shelves above the television, and several sumptuous exhibition catalogues. Behind the front door was a print from his favourite show, two years old now.

Yes: the heart of the city. He nodded, reassuring himself. Things were definitely falling into place. Things would fall into place. It took time. He was getting to know people. There were some familiar faces. He'd always been a little awkward, of course. But at least he knew that. At least he was aware of it.

The wind was getting colder. He pushed his hands deeper into his pockets, glad that he wasn't clutching a chilled carton of milk. The year's last leaves twitched and staggered across his path. He stepped into the deep shadow at the base of his building, let himself in and took the echoing steps up to his level. Below, he heard movement – a neighbour returning – and hurried on, unwilling to entangle himself in small talk. He was already holding the sharp knot of his keys, and now he pulled them from his pocket.

His walkway was deserted. He glanced down across the concourse below, but saw no one. He reached his door and felt himself relax, comforted as always by the familiar. Through the small frosted window beside the door, he made out the spiny leaves of the cactus on the sill above the telephone. Beside it, the grey rectangle of the frame showing the photo of his sister atop Scafell Pike to his empty flat.

Leaves skittered along the walkway behind him. He heard the wind career between the buildings. And beyond that, beyond the damp chill of the empty walkway and the great grey walls of the estate, he heard the low hum of the city, like the dying roar of a distant thunderstorm.

He saw the faint glow of the night reflected in the dull brass of his doorknob. A shadow passed over it, and his nose wrinkled at a sudden peculiar odour: something heavy and powerfully chemical. Simon began to turn, seeing a swift movement at his side, knowing at last that someone was there, feeling panic flutter in his chest. He sensed the man's height, saw a charcoal-coloured sleeve, and felt his stomach lurch with understanding. Then the clamp of wadding to his face. The iron band of an arm around him. He heard his keys drop to the floor. A powerful hand pinned him close. A dense, cloying fog descended. Pinpricks of light swarmed in his vision. His limbs grew heavy. The fog thickened in his head and a low voice somewhere in the night said: "Now you can rest."

Spirituous

Elise Valmorbida

He is out of bed at four o'clock in the morning, as usual. He scrubs, shaves, prays. The world is full of darkness. When he slips on his shoes he feels a flicker of satisfaction: his shoes are parallel, no left, no right. It doesn't matter which shoe his foot finds. It doesn't matter if it is dark. His feet will walk straight, straight and narrow. Across the world if God wills it. Captain James Cook is at this very moment braving wild seas in another hemisphere.

He kneels. The wood is uneven. No matter. He is in his eighth decade but he still enjoys rude health: keen knees, good skin, sound sleep. He feels no anxiety. This life is insubstantial as foam.

He says a prayer for the blessed soul of his mother. She did not bend. When his father was away, she preached – despite her sex – because there was not one man who could read a sermon without spoiling it.

He will start preaching at five o'clock, as usual. His crowds are larger even than his mother's. He uses no ornaments, no devices. Just obvious, easy, common words, the ordinary way of speaking. He will sing his brother's hymns to the very last word. He doesn't like things unfinished.

There is a fellow on the street outside, gurgling one minute, bleating and crying the next. His voice is disembodied in the darkness. The lamplighter has not been.

The earth shall reel to and fro like a drunkard.

Wood is uneven, but knees are hard, and feet are parallel. It is no hardship to abstain from idle songs. Or to refrain from talking in a merry, gay, diverting manner. Or to refuse spirituous liquors. He is bound to this plain hard ship that braves the wine-dark turbulence.

For forty years he has been preaching this strictness of life and he has not wavered. He has not bent. He has a message from God to all men.

–O–

Sulphur-crested cockatoos rock and screech on the flimsy tips of silver birches, playing with gravity. In the shade below, I am sharpening pencils for Miss Dorothy. The task is taking a long time. The longer I take, the longer I can avoid playing the piano. Miss Dorothy's pencils are getting shorter and shorter. I am turning them into demi-semi-quavers. I wonder if she will notice.

I stop for a rest. I breathe, a breve, another. The air is tangy with eucalyptus. I turn, turn, sharpen some more. The paint-edged shavings are turning, curling, breaking, returning home to mulch. Butterflies are not tricked. Bees are not tempted. Cicadas hide silently, pale green, waiting for twilight before playing their brash music. The pencils are suspiciously short. I have to go in.

And all the world went gay, went gay,

For half an hour in the street today!

Miss Dorothy asks me to place the stresses on the words. This is easy. I tap out the rhythm. Easier than piano keys. My hands are poised to play. I think of hanging spiders, rag mops. I am seated at the piano, my feet are parallel and Miss Dorothy sits beside me at an angle. She plays my thigh with her arthritic fingers. This is a demonstration of how my fingers should attack the hard ivory keys of the piano.

"Think of a sponge!" she urges me.

I think of cake, sea creatures, the kitchen sink. The thought is not helpful. I'd never do that to a sponge. My tomboy thigh is softer than a keyboard, harder than a sponge. Piano does not come easily to me, despite my hand-span which is already wider than an octave. I crash through the Teddy Bears' Picnic. I am crushed by the Linden Tree. I want to unlock the metronome and play with it, forget the piano. I like the word metronome. It sounds cosy and hollow at the same time.

Miss Dorothy is a spinster. I think the word spinster is harder than ivory, less beautiful. When people say the word I can hear the insult hiding inside. Every Miss should become a Mrs before too long. There are hands with wedding rings, or not. Girls show off engagement rings and other girls touch their fingers, gasp in admiration. I prefer the word spinet for Miss Dorothy. Her hands are old and knuckly and her rings are purely ornamental. Miss Dorothy is a spinet.

One day, despite everything, I arrive for my piano lesson early. I have to wait. There is a boy before me, one of those quiet pale-skinned English sorts who never question teachers. Every Good Boy Deserves Favour. Sometimes I wish I could be that good, but he must burn badly in the sun. He makes no mistakes. He's been practising his scales. Not once does Miss Dorothy say to him, "Oh, for crying out loud."

One day, I arrive more than usually late. From outside, I can hear Miss Dorothy playing. The piano is taking deep breaths and laughing, booming, singing, rolling, sighing. I can picture Miss Dorothy's arthritic hands running up and down the keyboard like two spotted crabs. The music they make is beautiful. I can't hear the click of her varnished nail-tips. I've never heard her play before, just little runs of demonstration notes. I realise I must be punishment to her ears once a week. I'm ashamed of the stubby pencils, but there's no way round it.

I wait at the back door. The magpies are gurgling. The crows sound like baby lambs, children crying. I peer through the fly-wire to the gloomy corridor inside. I stand, waiting. A spider has woven white fuzz in the screen's torn edge. Where Miss Dorothy's handwritten note is stuck to the latch, the sticky tape is turning brown, clear and fragile as a discarded cicada shell clinging by its claws to bark.

CLOSE THE DOOR! the note says in curly writing, all capitals awash with swashes. I think of Queen Elizabeth's signature. She danced on Walter Raleigh's cape and never wet one slipper. I saw her initials on a TV ad, writing themselves, no hand. She had more curls to her name than letters. I think of bath foam, whipped cream. After the Aborigines, men in capes discovered Australia. They cruised along its curves like mosquitoes looking for an inlet. They called it New South Wales or New Holland, but secretly it was older than anywhere, so old it had no quakes or live volcanoes, no pulse at all, just dust and skin.

I open the back door as quietly as I can. Fly-wire doors always make a noise. They screech or croak like birds. Miss Dorothy's music is dancing down her corridor, filling all the spaces tight as cake-mix in a tin, filling me with wishfulness: I wish I could play piano like Miss Dorothy but I know I never will. I let the screen door close behind me. Gently. The crabs are still scuttling side-ways, left and right, joints clicking, tickling the blacks, pressing the whites, releasing chords so complicated I can hear a web of instruments, not just one.

Miss Dorothy has a sister spinster, and the difference between them, I think, is a pin. When Miss Dorothy plays the piano, you can hear a pin drop. Or a back door close.

The note on the latch is for her sister, who is deaf (which is why the words must be capitalised) and forgetful (which is why there are notes everywhere). GO TO BACK DOOR! HANG UP PHONE! DO NOT REMOVE DOILY! Her sister is deaf, silent, invisible. She sifts about on thin carpet, boils water, exists in other rooms where piano pupils do not go. I have seen her only fleetingly, slight as a startled beetle whose screen has been snatched away.

I move slowly down the corridor, tiptoe inch by inch to the piano-room door. It's like playing statues. The longer I take, the longer I can hear the music Miss Dorothy makes, stave off the noise I will make, not wishing to punish her. At last I enter.

"I didn't think you were coming," she says, unsmiling.

She stops. Gets up. Sits herself on her usual seat. At an angle, to the side. Ready for another lesson.

The session begins as usual and then it continues. I haven't been practising. I know the beginnings of everything, but that's all. Through repetition, my hands have memorised the first sequence of steps. I've been reading a story about a blind girl who says that finger-tips contain grey matter just like brains, that even when the brain is damaged, fingers remember. I stumble through The Can-Can.

Miss Dorothy sells sheet music to me at the price she paid for it, always a matter of cents. She buys it from a famous music shop in town called Brash's, which should sell cockatoos or fly-wire doors, not rhapsodies and symphonies with curly titles from Old Europe. The music is specially adapted for children (not too many black notes, no ornaments) and Miss Dorothy uses any one of her fine collection of sharp pencils to number the notes so that I don't run out of fingers. Her numerals are as beautiful as her capitals.

"Oh, for crying out loud," she says when I play and run out of fingers. There's no way round it. I wish I had six.

One day after school I catch her at the greengrocer's. Off guard. She hardly says hello. She buys a single potato, a couple of carrots, one banana. I want to laugh. My mother doesn't. Later she tells me the word frugal.

At Christmas I give Miss Dorothy a special fruit cake in a tin, imported all the way from England. My mother bought it from my father's shop, and I know it's a matter of dollars not cents. Miss Dorothy unwraps her gift, carefully peeling off the sticky tape so that she can reuse the paper.

Her powdered face, all soft and pouchy, breaks into a smile. Her teeth are sudden yellow like old, old ivory – but they are neat and parallel, unlike mine. She reads the title on the tin: Old-Fashioned Luxury Christmas Cake. The swashes curl about and fill the space as elegantly as any queen. She lifts her glasses (she wears them on a necklace chain) and her eyes grow large like moist grey oysters in their pointed pink frames. Silently she reads. Her powdery cheeks drop and her teeth disappear again as her lips purse.

"Oh no, I can't accept this," she says, holding it out to me. "You'll have to take it back."

I am astonished. That's the word children always are in books. Astonished.

At Weddings, Easters, Bar Mitzvahs, First Communions, Name Days, Christenings, Birthday Parties, Christmases – I have never ever heard anyone say no to a present. I have never seen anyone, young or old, give a present back. Aren't presents what every person lives for? Dreams about? I am astonished.

"Why not?" I ask, reluctantly taking the cake.

"It's got brandy in it."

"Where?" I search for brandy. There's the incriminating word. I've tasted it. My mother puts it in the sauce for calf's liver. The pudding. Trifle. I like it.

"Dried fruits soaked in brandy." Miss Dorothy points. Her varnished nail-tips click on tin.

"But it's just the fruits," I say, as if I can convince her of something. There's all that flour and fat and goodness. What's wrong with brandy?

"It's against my religion."

"What religion?" I ask. The present is pressing on my thighs.

"Methodist."

That's a word I don't know. I think of a saying my mother has: *there's method in my madness.* I think of the poorest drunks, the ones who can't afford beer or wine. They have methylated spirits.

Miss Dorothy is dead. I walk up City Road from Moorgate, playing scales on the piano in my head. The plain hard ship of Methodism crossed the world from here.

John Wesley is buried in unconsecrated ground, but the place is blessed by his bones. He sleeps soundly, as he did in life. His feet are parallel. He does not bend. Here is his house and here is his chapel, both built perfectly plain. He is not to know that others after him have added their curls and swashes, their ornaments and devices. Across the road in Bunhill Fields lies his mother, who preached despite her sex. She is at home with the crowd of Dissenters and Non-Conformists who dared to preach in the open air, now silent, now mulch.

25 —
TO HERE
MOORGATE

Some arrivals & departures

Tom Lynham

This is how it will happen. Circle Line. Liverpool Street. 7.16 a.m. Half asleep. Platform is a rugby scrum. Teetering on the edge. Dangerous territory. We've all been there. Mutant mice scurry around the live rail. Frantically late. The train rumbles in and grinds to a halt. The racket eviscerates my hangover. Squeeeeze into carriage. Airless. Breathless. Elbows jag into necks. Groins grind into bums. Grab at the handrail. Middle finger jams in sliding doors. Oh-fuck... Yank it out. *FINGERFUCKINGTIP MISSING!* Blood splatters shirts and ties. Stick stump in mouth and scream FUCK! Try it. Strangely painless. Dribbling like cartoon vampire. My favourite hand. An exclusion zone will materialise around me. Then some angel pulls the emergency handle. Train judders. Doors crank open. Smother stump with hanky. A fist of crimson candyfloss. I imagine tearing up the escalator past a blur of cheesy advertising models with chewing gum noses.

Rush into the heaving concourse of the main line station. Out of the darkness and into the light. Shafts of sunshine dazzle down from the crystal roof. A cathedral of collisions; of gothic detail, of digital information, of screaming retail brands, of people from every race, nationality, class, culture, creed and who-knows-what sexual persuasions. Part of me will be going into shock. Part of me will be trying to think rationally; think A&E, think ambulance, think next of kin. But I'll be swept along on tides of humanity; workers & skivers, day trippers & train spotters, beggars & scoundrels, pick pockets & ticket scammers; the itinerant and nomadic tribes that wash in and out of here every day. It will become impossible to move in a straight line. I see myself crashing into a tribe of American evangelists in sharp black suits bound for the airport with badges proclaiming *Hi! I'm Cy from Miami! Praise the Lord!* Outside the Easy-Walk-In-Tanning-Kiosk, I crunch into a gaggle of Essex girls with bronzed skin, snippety legs and diamanté belly buttons. I'll be herded into Boots and collide with a teenage mother pushing two spitting toddlers who eyeball my injury with Midwich Cuckoo stares. I'll tumble over suitcases, scatter florists displays, skid into scalding cappuccinos, wrestle with flexible queuing systems, emasculate small dogs and banjax signing systems.

I attempt to tack a haphazard course to the station entrance, but the faster I move the slower I go. By now, the blood loss will be making me feel woozy, but then a pair of friendly arms will envelop me, like landing on a cloud of cotton wool. Focusing, I'll look up and see the face of a saint, her shimmering halo glowing like a Belisha beacon. Am I in Heaven? And she is going to smile back, a beatific grin that evaporates my anxiety. At this point, the rest of the station goes into slow motion, as if we are suspended in some once-removed dimension. And from this place of safety I'll dare to ask who she is. She will inspect my throbbing hand,

and tell me without a whiff of irony that she is Saint Mechteld, the patron saint of missing fingers. Programmed by years of religious iconography I'll look for iridescent robes, celestial trappings, perhaps a pearly harp, or a lute, or a flute, or a magical singing lyre or even a pouting cherub. But she wears Calvin Klein this, Tommy Hilfiger that, FCUK something else and sports a pair of scruffy Nike Air Zooms. Over her shoulder is a zippered bag with Amsterdam-Schiphol flight tags. Mechteld will tell me in perfect English, with only an inflection of Dutch that she's just arrived on the Stansted Express. And I hear myself splutter stupid questions like: How did you know I would do it? Can you get my finger back? Why didn't you stop me? But she will simply whistle through her front teeth, remove a spliff from behind her ear, and plant it between my lips like a shut-your-gob thermometer.

Aided and abetted by an aura of Lebanese gold, she will spirit me out of the station, floating up the escalators into the frantic streets of the City. As we hit the open air, I discover her perfect halo is little better than the glitter and fuse wire constructions we made for our Christmas tree fairy when we were kids. She appears underslept and overworked. Her fingernails are almost nibbled down to the cuticle. But for all this mortal vulnerability, she will exude an ethereal credulity. Then forcing my hand above my head like a red flag, she will steer me through the secretaries, receptionists, managers and personal assistants as they are gobbled up by the office buildings. We'll slip down the ancient lanes and dog-leg alleys to a Tower Hamlets Health Authority building I've never noticed before, with a sign outside announcing the Liverpool Street Finger Clinic.

In reception, a triage nurse who obviously knows Mechteld well, peeps under the sodden wrapping to ascertain the extent of the damage, then logs my details. Our entry to the outpatients' waiting room is greeted with cheers of recognition by finger victims whom Mechteld has helped in the past. Some wear slings supporting heavily bandaged, half-cocked arms. Some hold pinned and wired fingers aloft like reluctant pupils in a detention class. Others are just popping in for post-op check-ups, and quietly appreciating their mending fingers like never before. Mechteld's presence warms them up, and knuckle-biting narratives of industrial accidents and unfortunate occurrences trundle round the room – everyone has a story to tell: Egbert Monchique sliced his fingers off with a DeWalt radial arm saw at the City & Guilds Apprentice Centre just around the corner. We cringe as Mechteld recalls him carrying the tips to the clinic like fairground goldfish in a plastic bag. He says the surgeons worked through the night to glue them back on fuelled by fixes of Mars bars and Tizer. Johnny Toronto tells us he works for a geophysical exploration outfit on the 37th floor of the Broadgate Centre above the station. Three months ago he lost his little finger to a maverick detonator during a seismic survey in Azerbaijan. He's here today because a slip on the Millennium Ice Rink has opened up the old wound again. Nasimah from the Bangalorious Fashion Emporium in Petticoat Lane had her index finger amputated after mangling it in the cogs of a Singer hydraulic steam press. Jean-Patrice d'Allery, from a Parisienne dynasty of master wood carvers has restored Grinling Gibbons' masterpieces all over the Parish of Bishopsgate. Jean is a regular at the clinic having whittled away most of his fingers over the years. Albion Milton, the septuagenarian Master at Arms of the Bunhill Fields Burial Grounds severed his ring finger when removing William & Catherine Blake's restless tombstone during the refurbishment of the unisex public toilets. Hanna Hilb rescued a fox that was hit by a bus right outside the main station and took it back to the Museum of Immigration in the old Huguenot quarter of Spitalfields where she is a curator. But the ungrateful beast attacked her, bit off her middle finger and then stole a chicken from the Three Monkeys Curry House in Brick Lane. Charles Crispin runs a veneer warehouse in Patina Yard, Hoxton. He shredded his left thumb while quarter cutting a burl of precious thuya from the foothills of the Atlas Mountains. He proudly holds up his transplanted big left toe for all to admire, which now flourishes on the space his thumb vacated.

Visits to hospitals confront us with our ephemerality. As we tread limbo in corridors and cubicles, I'll ask Mechteld how she got the gig to be a patron saint. She'll explain that Liverpool Street is twinned with Amsterdam Centraal station and they enjoy reciprocal patron saint arrangements. She says fingers are in her blood and that she comes from a long line of fingery heroes. Her great, great grandfather Joop was the boy who stuck his legendary finger in the Domberg Dyke and saved the village from drowning. Her cousin

Geertje's family have been manufacturing the world famous Gouda cheeses for generations, and every hallmark hole is still gouged by their stiff Lutheran fingers. Back in the early seventeenth century, Mechteld's green-fingered ancestor Jochem Hoogaboom, hand-reared the very first tulip bulbs that triggered the tulip mania, that lead to the crash of the Amsterdam stock exchange.

Mechteld will tell me that anyone can become a patron saint: choose your cause and apply for the vocation. The training is not dissimilar to The Knowledge – the competency test for London taxi drivers. But instead of practising how to get from A to B, you learn how to navigate fate and fortune. There's not much money in it, but the job satisfaction is beyond measure. Mechteld cautions that in these times of universal diaspora, compulsory multi-tasking and diminishing attention spans, we all need someone to look over our shoulder.

While positioning my hand for X-ray, Mechteld will confront me with my collision and question whether it was really even an accident. Once the film is processed, we pore over my ghostly skeleton. We stare at the missing fingertip; this intrinsic part of me that does not exist anymore. Mechteld observes that for many of her customers, the accident is often an unconscious cry for help; the body mutinies against the errant ego and attempts to return it to the fold. At first I'll feel hostile to such a suggestion, because I've always believed in the supremacy of mind over matter. But she will couch her arguments in such intriguing and unthreatening terms, I'll begin to see right through my defences. We'll talk so effortlessly, I'll find myself admitting to vulnerabilities I wouldn't dare share with others; that my life has been like a dog chasing its tail; that I've never given much thought to where I was going or why.

A nurse will appear and show us into a small specialist operating theatre with anatomical charts of hands, tendons and nerves on the walls. She sets out plastic sheets, kidney bowls, scalpels, forceps, tweezers and swabs on an orthopaedic trauma table. While waiting for the surgeon, Mechteld and I shall reflect on our progress through life, and the difference between what could have happened, and what did. We'll talk about what's true – and what's not true, and how through failure or disappointment, some people turn their lives into elaborate fictions.

Dr Bethiana Sanchez – on secondment from Hospital del Dedo Sagrado in Barcelona – breezes in like a mother hen surrounded by a flock of medical students. She is delighted to see Mechteld and they embrace like old friends. She inspects the remainder of my finger and instructs the surgical nurse to administer a local anaesthetic. As the needles go in, Mechteld slides her arm round my shoulder. The doctor talks the procedure through as she sews up the blood vessels, pulls the muscle over the bone, folds the skin into a neat flap and stitches everything together. After dressings, tetanus jab, antibiotics and an appointment for tomorrow, I am let out on probation.

As we emerge onto the steps of the clinic it is clear that something has happened between us. It's incredibly tangible but impossible to articulate. We have been manoeuvring towards it since the moment we met, and it feels exhilaratingly awkward.

Wafts of lunch from numerous cafes aggravate our hunger and we walk back towards Liverpool Street and the Great Eastern Hotel, a terracotta temple to the glory of rail travel. We hog a squashy leather sofa in the Fishmarket Bar, sip pints of medicinal Guinness and talk about the power of fingers and how they are taken so for granted. Mechteld touches my cheek and says fingers are sense organs, a kind of radar, antennae, existential measuring sticks. She clenches her glass and describes fingers as the tools of the hunter-gatherer, designed to catch, select, shape and make their mark. Gathering momentum, she'll talk excitedly about how we use our fingers to communicate, and with animated gestures, act out the universal signs – pointing, warning, beckoning and ticking off. She'll poke out her tongue and sneak in a V sign and I'll instinctively counter with a fist. Then suddenly, giggling like kids we are playing Rock Paper Scissors and the kiss just happens. It startles us but feels alarmingly natural. And then the kisses will come rapidly and spontaneously as if our lips were made for each other.

Our destination for the rest of the afternoon is inevitable, but we need fuel to get us there and find a table in the art deco Aurora Dining Rooms. There is a delicious sense of erotic anticipation as we gorge ourselves on regional dishes expressed into Liverpool Street from all over East Anglia: Butley native oysters dredged from the brackish creeks of Orford Ness. Toad in the Hole made from Norfolk Old Spot porkers reared in Great Snoring with heaps of juicy samphire from Wells-next-the-Sea. And finally Walberswick fudge cake, dripping with sheep's yoghurt from Suffolk ewes grazed on the Blythburgh flood meadows.

Over espresso and armagnac, Mechteld tells me she is being relocated. The world is changing fast and there are new insecurities for patron saints to address such as self-help groups, international terrorism, cigarette smoking and genetic engineering. She says one of her friends is now the Greek patron saint of mobile phones. Mechteld has been offered postings in South America; maybe Chile, maybe Honduras, maybe Brazil. But she'll add that she's not decided anything about her future…yet.

Then we check into the hotel and take the glass lift to the seventh floor. The luxurious room is set into the eaves and oriel windows peep out over leaded roofs, flagpoles and church spires towards Threadneedle Street. We'll wash away all the crap and crud of the day in a scalding power-shower – my bandages protected by a pedal bin liner – and collapse on the fresh linen sheets. One handed, I'll feel clumsy, an awkward sexuality, my fingers like blunt instruments without any sensitivity. But Mechteld's fingers are exquisitely tuned. They have a phenomenal touch; like hummingbird's sneezes, like a kitten's inquisitiveness, like peals of laughter. And I'll learn so much from her. My fingers will find a new voice and we shall tease and tickle and stroke and squeeze each other into a frenzy of pleasure.

Afterwards, clinging close, as naked as you can get, we'll listen to the muffled drone of the traffic and the whine of jets limbering up for Heathrow. The rumbling of Tube trains way down below will shudder up through the fabric of the building. I'll slip into the deepest sleep and wake hours later.

Mechteld has gone but her halo reclines on the pillow, with a small note in spidery handwriting, asking me never to forget what happened to us today, and to light the occasional candle for her.

A correlation of ghosts

Rishi Dastidar

here, the edge of a city; this is my land.

I am Botolph, a missionary who seeks to give succour to all those who find themselves travelling. And here I will begin to timber a place for those ending, those beginning their journeys.

A place for outcasts, where they can pray afore they go, or after they arrive. A place for those in transit. A place for those who are transient.

This will be not no-man's-land, but everyman's land; a place where the disposed and dispossessed can feel belonging again, not tied to the land but granted a sense of solace before starting out to wherever they might go. No longer walking with the dead.

Following the example of Christopher, I will continue to preach the gospel wherever God's will takes me. I have seen Gaul; I am a Saxon; I am a Celt. I have been a monk. I have lived and taught according to Benedict's principles. My monastery is far to the north, in a place the locals have taken to calling Botolph's town – a joke, I think.

I have saved many. I have been a witness to miracles. I have shown many how to make miracles from the lives that we, that they, are given.

After near threescore years, soon I will no longer be here; but here I will remain. I will be buried in many places. In death I will be found everywhere and yet nowhere, forever restless, forever being taken wherever the Lord wills.

And everywhere, I shall endure.

I have been meek so you need not be, I have starved so you need not go hungry, I have faced danger so you may be safe.

I will look after you no matter who you might be and no matter where

–O–

gate! And open it now! Or we the mighty shall tear it down brick by brick!

We've taken Colchester, we've taken Manningtree. Essex burns with this injustice, this latest *demand.* Enough. And we say, "Enough!" In our name, in the name of the people, the peas-ants, we will take you, this city. Starting here. We will start here.

We ain't here by choice or by accident. Our God's will has taken us. Aelgate is free and open for all, for all us free men, from all time. It will never be closed again. You're the purveyors of evil here. We shall take it back from you Customs-House clerks and Excise fuckknaves who hide inside. Stones and locks will not protect you from this fire, our will, God's will.

We're here because we've been driven, driven to it. We ain't no rebels. We're the King's loyal servants who've been betrayed by disloyal leaders, bloated corrupt captains abroad who do nothing, *nothing!* to protect us from the French, threats near us, thieves pretending, pretending to be our government at home.

Our current condition, our unfair condition, can't be found in our holy gospels. You've taxed us the most heavily, too heavily. We won't give you a penny for this unfair toll, not now, not ever. This will be the last, the last of these outrageous demands.

And this summer day we will inflame the city, free our broth-ers from your bonds, the same demands you place on us, against the will of God, the word of God.

We won't be serfs no longer, we'll be free tenants and our rents limited. We want the heads of the extravagant, those murderous traitors Sudbury, Hales, John of Gaunt, around our most noble lord, the King His Majesty.

And we shan't accept no lordship save that of our king. We won't be oppressed by

–O–

, almost; well, well, it is this London, this neighbourhood, this very ward no less, that has raised me, and I want to celebrate it with you.

I was baptised at that handsome, bold church that you can see on the corner. In my long – and some might say, modestly successful – time I have been, as well as others, the alderman for Portsoken, the member of the loyal parliament for the City. And I address you all this day not just as a proud old member of the Carpenter's Company, but also the proud old son of a carpenter. A man proud for what you have given him, the . . . the support during the exercise of his public life.

And so I wish to give back as much as I can in the few short years I have left to me. And so today, the first small step in my road to charity. We gather here to endow a school, my school, the Cass school – a school in which the knowledge that shall be taught will be that knowledge of the Christian religion according to the principles of the Church of England.

Now, some of you ward members, parishioners or indeed other naysayers far less generous than you might be might cast doubt as to why I have chosen to found this particular school. Some might unkindly say that it is to defray a small whisper of sin that is attached to my name and my friendships. A form of penance. As if my record of supporting the church and its party in parliament is not proof enough for these foul whisperers!

But no, no . . . I can assure you that all I want is to give back, and improve the area in which I have lived and will continue to live until it is willed otherwise, and which I have served loyally for all my public life.

And indeed, I hope that this school outlives me. Even more, I hope that the principles that it stands for outlive me, and support the establishment of trade and all the other commercial arts across the City.

This place, where we have known fear, decay and death, is what we want to change. And education is where

–O–

all join us today, on this most special of days. It is a fine way to see in this new year of our Lord sixteen hundred and eighty-four, is it not?

Mary and I, and the rest of the Defoe family, are delight'd to be marry'd here in this Parish of Botolph, this fine Church with six strong bells; and this Parish will be the place where we establish our home and business, where we begin our lives in the eyes of God. I am so very glad that in Mary I have found such a partner in the battle against the wilderness of this world.

And is it not fitting, with what *some* might call my *Nonconformist* background, that we have achiev'd this union in a church with a resolute history of supporting independent thought, a freedom of conscience unmatched elsewhere in this City? It is a proud record, and this may be the only Pulpit that I might consider to call my office.

I am fortunate in having a father prominent in the civic and commercial life of this City, and I hope that I will follow as successfully in his footsteps. I start as a young man, as a wholesale hosier, but I can see the future of trade opening up to me, as it does to the rest of this City: tobacco, logwoods, wines, spirits, cloth. And factories further down the muddy artery that is the river; and maybe even Contraptions and Speculations as yet undreamt of by the imaginations of our age.

And it will be this trade, this Commerce, that gives our time, our Nation, unrivalled power, unmatched importance and influence on the affairs of Men and the affairs of the World. It is how we will continue to rebuild this city after the depredations of fire and plague. For London is a great body which *circulates* all, *exports* all, and at last *pays* for all. We must wear this influence well and lightly; but wear it we

–O–

illusionist, madam? What rot, I cry! I am not a professor of hairdressing, or a dancing master! I am the renowned *Dr* Henry Pepper! I am a fellow of the Chemical Society, an engineer no less! What you will see is not hocus-pocus, no sir, no madam! Rather, this is the latest that the leading scientists of our age, physicists, chemists, engineers, have laboured to produce.

And what a device, what a marvel! Maybe you have seen it at the polytechnic on Regent Street, but I could think of no greater location to bring it to than here, a place where I know ghosts roam. And I know that many of you in the audience will have seen spirits abroad!

Ladies and gentlemen, this evening we are gathered on the site of one of London's most notorious burial grounds. Within this very churchyard where we stand lie over 5,000 poor unfortunate souls who fell victim to the vilest and most rabid of pestilences that stalked this land in the year of our Lord sixteen hundred and sixty-five.

And you know, good burghers of Aldgate, that your land is one of ghouls and the undead, those poor and forsaken. And when it rains, when the ground is soaked, and when it is dark, when the spirits rouse themselves on All Hallows' Eve and haunt the living, people are afraid. And this is such a night!

And though you may gather not knowing what may happen here, be not afraid! On this breeding-ground for ghosts, through my device, we shall capture one such restless soul and show you that it is not to be feared! Not so, not at all! A beautiful, haunting remnant of times past, waiting, writhing in silent, endless agony. Now, behold this real play

–O–

Kate just Kate yeah I live round here work round here play round here die round here you have a firm chest don't say much do you? you were chatty earlier what's happened fuck I ain't no dipper I ain't no harlot no buttered bun I do used to write books sell books about famous people famous people what been hung as well do you still want business a four-penny knee-trembler so I can gets me lodging look at the fruit in my bonnet its as pretty as my face you like my hazel eyes my auburn hair not here its too dark down here and it stinks lets go somewhere else scared after all the murders round here not me I've been round here for seven years now I know my way around I was in the nick earlier tonight those peelers don't like me doing fire engines down the street do they then I laid down in the street to have a little sleep they said I was drunk I was causing them entertainment I'm a good woman a good woman who's bettering herself to earn the money to see my family again to show 'em that I am a good person that I don't just drink and all looking for a bit of fun that's all they told me I should stick by the church to meet my *friends* but that'd be boring wouldn't I ain't a nothing I think the police they're hunting me I'm the hunted for them maybe you'll be famous one day we'll be

–O–

about. We stand out all on our own. A bit isolated, really, apart from anything else. Not surprising. Have a look at your Tube map. You'll have to look twice to find us. You could airbrush us out and no one would be any the wiser. We're neither here nor there. We're not Tower Hill, we're not Liverpool Street. Just that bit in between. And the end of a line as well. But Metroland doesn't count, does it?

But I guess that makes sense. After all, the Circle doesn't exist, so why should the stations? Yeah, that's right, it doesn't exist. It's a virtual line, a virtual network. Ghost carriages running on other people's tracks, something like that. Only the bends are ours. And even they don't work properly.

We do have a function. Loads of lines out to and back from the east converge round here. So we have to make sure that things come in safely. And go out safely as well.

Is it scary to work here? Not really, but we do have our own ghost about: a grey-haired old lady who's supposed to be our guardian angel. In the fifties, we had an electrician doing some work on the track over that way. One of my predecessors, he looked over and saw this old woman stroking the man's hair as he worked.

Next second, whoosh, guy gets electrocuted. Twenty-two thousand volts straight through him. Knocked unconscious, but would you believe that was it? Nothing else. No burns, no scratches, no nothing. So yeah, she's our guardian angel ghost.

Nah, I've never seen her.

Oh, the log book? Well, it's a great rumour. Is it true? That we keep a record of all the odd goings-on that we see or the passengers hear? Footsteps when there's no one else around, that sort of thing?

I couldn't tell you (smiles).

Yeah, spooky round

MARK LANE (FORMER NAME OF TOWER HILL)

You are here

Karen McCarthy

In the city of my birth I am a stranger.
I am one with the shoals of tourists who circle
The Tower, looking for life in a ghost
town. We swallow ancient stone churches,
wash them down with ravenous mouthfuls of river
and overpriced portions of fish and chips: whole.

If I can unwrap the past it will be whole
underneath the paper, shiny and stranger
than anything that ever swam in the river.
I have been searching for an old Circle
Line station. I looked in several churches.
I found an angry gargoyle, interviewed a ghost.

A word of advice: when interviewing a ghost
make sure you have sharp pencils and a whole
notebook to hand. Ghosts hang around old churches,
bored and hungry for company. They'll tell a stranger
their life story. Twice. These types go full circle.
Believe me, they're more slippery than a river.

Mark Lane station used to face the river.
It was not always a forgotten ghost.
Platforms busy with people, it was a circle
on the map. It had a timetable whole
lives revolved around and daily, one stranger
would greet another, like they did in the churches.

All Hallows is one of those City churches:
now parishioners number two. The river
slips across its boundaries. Each year is stranger.
A boy comes and beats the water and ghost
stations sing in the choir. Trains choo choo whole
hymns. He beats the boundary, she casts the circle.

I stand on top of Tower Hill, in the circle
of the sundial that tells of time and churches.
I have been underground and emerged whole.
I have thrown the yellow past into the river.
I know how to make friends with a ghost.
My city is no longer a stranger.

The river of time is really no stranger
than a talkative ghost, or even a whole
stone circle of old city churches.

Notes and findings

1. Mark Lane station always had a bit of sibling rivalry with its
sister station, Tower Hill. The whole thing started when it opened in
1882 as Tower of London. The Metropolitan Railway and the Metropolitan District Railway (think the Judean People's Front versus
the People's Front of Judea) had some sort of administrative barney
about who should finish the Circle Line and where (details of which
can be found in Jim E. Connor's useful book *London's Disused
Underground Stations*, Capital Transport Publishing, 2001). As a
result, the Tower of London reopened as Mark Lane on 6 October
1884. The victory lasted a whole 62 years, until the station was
renamed Tower Hill on 1 September 1946. It was closed and resited
on 4 February 1967, and has been Tower Hill ever since.

2. For the most part, the Mark Lane entrance was on Byward
Street at a site currently occupied by an All Bar One. A subway on
this stretch gives access to the old station forecourt. Downstairs

is dark and grimy, but seemingly free of litter, rats and – stranger still – mice. It is spooky by torchlight. At street level, the bar next door (now closed) used to cellar its wine in one of the back rooms. A few fading ads are left on the wall, notably one from the employment agency Alfred Marks's "In the pink" campaign back in 1967, when every Chelsea girl was a temp. A black-and-white graffito tag from 2001 adorns the disused platform. You can see the brightly lit trains full of passengers who can't see you as they pass through on their way to Tower Hill.

3. Mark Lane was situated in the parish of All Hallows Church. Today the parish has just two resident parishioners (and, as the helpful vicar told me, they live in the church). The parish is not particularly large, but at one point it runs down to the middle of the River Thames. The parishioners still observe the ancient tradition of beating the bounds of the parish with sticks. Leaving no boundary unbeaten, they go out in a boat, and a small boy (from All Hallow's School, apparently) is hung overboard by his feet to beat the water.

4. Another interesting church in the vicinity is St Olave's on Hart Street. It was much loved by Samuel Pepys, who was buried there. It dates back to around 1450, and is one of only eight churches to have survived the Great Fire of London in 1666. It has a pretty little churchyard; don't be put off by the skulls on top of the gate. Dickens was another literary fan, calling it St Ghastly Grim on account of this macabre decoration.

5. The best river tour is on the Circular Tours boat the *Suerita*, which runs from Tower Pier to Westminster in a relatively straight line (rather than a circle as the name suggests). The tour guides are keen to remind you they're working boat crew, not professionals. This means the voices are real not recordings, the info "may or may not be accurate," and the jokes are funny.

6. The Beefeaters live in the walls of the Tower of London. They have their own padre, a ghost or two, and an on-site doctor. The ravens live in cages, but are allowed out. Whether they are true monarchists is uncertain. They stay because one wing is clipped; they can fly only in circles.

TOWER HILL

The unkindness
of ravens

Anelia Schutte

Restlessness drove them to the skies again.

Daphne du Maurier

The Ravenmaster was first to fall ill. Influenza, the Tower doctor said. Fever, cough, sore throat, aching muscles... all typical symptoms of your common or garden flu. A course of antibiotics and plenty of bed rest and he'd be as fit as his ravens in no time at all.

But the Ravenmaster's condition deteriorated fast, and by the third day his every breath was a painful, wheezing gasp. To add to the doctor's concern, all four of the Ravenmaster's assistants were laid low with similar symptoms, confined to their rooms in the Tower like the prisoners of old.

The ambulances came that evening, when the tourists and their cameras had long gone. Only the Tower ravens watched as their master and his assistants were taken away.

Over the weeks that followed, the remaining yeoman warders did what they could to look after the birds. But the ravens listened only to the Ravenmaster and would let no one else near them, pecking viciously at any hand that came too close. Left alone, though, the birds seemed happy enough. They gulped down the fresh meat left out by the warders each day, and hopped into their nesting boxes without coaxing at dusk. They were as mischievous as ever – especially Thor, who liked to pull up the gardener's freshly planted seedlings – but on the whole they were perfectly well behaved.

Until the time came to trim their wings.

The yeoman warders approached Matthew first, as he was the youngest and smallest of the six. Three warders, all strong men, closed in on the raven, their hands outstretched and ready to grab. But as soon as they got hold of the bird, he pecked at their faces, leaving them no choice but to drop his squirming black body to shield their eyes. The other five ravens were no less aggressive, and all three men came away with deep cuts to their arms and hands; one suffered a gash to his brow.

All too aware of the legend, but unable to approach the birds for fear of losing an eye, the yeoman warders abandoned their attempts to trim the ravens' wings. The birds were causing no trouble, and as long as they were fed regularly, they had no reason to leave, or so the warders reasoned. After all, where would they go?

And so the days passed, and the ravens' wings grew.

It was Matthew who first decided to test his newly developed lifting feathers. One moment he was hopping along the green among the visiting families and tour groups; the next he was flapping his wings and rising into the sky. He circled the Bloody Tower once, twice, three times, all the while calling to the magpies in the trees, the seagulls on the riverbank and the five landbound ravens below. In one swift movement, he swooped down towards Traitor's Gate, dipped his beak in the shallow water and ascended again to settle on top of St Thomas's Tower.

Bran and Munin soon followed. The two ravens spread their glimmering oil-slick wings and lifted their bodies into the air. They soared side by side above the White Tower, then separated and reunited again, catching the sunlight with every powerful flap of their wings.

The yeoman warders stopped and stared at the ravens in flight. When they looked at each other, there was fear in their eyes. The legend . . .

After their fleeting aerial display, Bran and Munin joined Matthew on St Thomas's Tower, where they huddled together as if conspiring. Just when the warders thought they might never come down, the ravens flapped their wings and glided back towards the green in a perfectly synchronised movement. There they remained for the rest of the day, dutifully retiring to their nesting boxes again at dusk.

From that day on, all six ravens frequently embarked on such brief flights, calling as they soared through the air. But they always remained within the Tower walls. Satisfied that the ravens would not fulfil the fateful prophecy, the yeoman warders resumed their daily duties with no more than an occasional glance at the birds.

The other birds came on a Friday.

It was an unusually quiet morning at the Tower as there was a big event elsewhere in London that day. Yet the occasional group of tourists still came to be entertained with tales of torture, murder and execution. It was around mid-morning when the warders first noticed the magpies in the leaning tree on the green; not just the pair that had been nesting there, but about a dozen of the black and white birds dotted among the branches.

One for sorrow, two for mirth...

With every moment that passed, more magpies flew in from beyond the Tower walls until the branches of every tree in the grounds were creaking under their collective weight.

Three for a wedding, four for a birth...

And still the birds came: not only magpies, but also rooks, jays and carrion crows; scores of birds that settled on the Wardrobe Tower, the Bell Tower and the Bloody Tower.

Five for silver, six for gold,
Seven for a secret not to be told...

The birds seemed intent on taking over every nook, cranny, windowsill and rooftop, save for the White Tower, on which only six birds were perched. From their vantage point, the Tower ravens watched as their kinfolk arrived.

Frightened by this ominous sight, the tourists huddled around the yeoman warders for reassurance. Was it normal for such vast numbers of birds to come to the Tower? Yes, yes, the warders lied. Magpies, jays, crows and rooks were common in these parts. They were probably trying to escape the commotion in town.

Eight for heaven, nine for hell
And ten for the devil's own sel'.

What the warders failed to mention was that the tourists were no longer the only foreigners there. Among the magpies, carrion crows, rooks and jays entering the Tower, there were now hooded crows. And ravens. Hundreds of them. They must have come from the moors, the Hebrides, the Pennines – places where they were naturally found. Places where they belonged.

Without a sound save the flapping of their great wings, the ravens settled on the outer walls until the Tower was surrounded by a moving, breathing barricade of black.

The warders ushered the tourists out of the gates, hushing the crying children and reassuring their agitated parents. The birds were harmless, they promised, but something must have scared them, so it would be best to leave them alone for a while.

As the warders closed the gates behind them, they became aware of an eerie silence. There were thousands of birds all around them: on the green, the trees, the rooftops, the walls and the windowsills. But they all sat perfectly still, staring, each and every one, at the six ravens on the White Tower.

Thor broke the silence. "Come on then," he called in the Ravenmaster's voice. He had learned to mimic his master years before, but never had his voice sounded so menacing. The other five ravens answered in unison, not in words, but in a loud, drawn-out *kraawk* that echoed between the Tower walls.

At once, Thor, Hugine, Bran, Mugin, Branwen and Matthew flapped their wings and took flight. They circled the White Tower over and over again, gradually widening the ring until they were tracing the Tower's outer walls in the sky. As if the six ravens were creating a whirlwind with their mighty wings, the other birds rose towards them, tens of thousands of wings flapping in a roaring crescendo.

The Tower ravens, now distinguishable from the others only by the rings around their legs, broke free from the frenzied mass of birds. When Thor, the last of the six, crossed the Tower walls, a low rumble sounded behind them. The White Tower was trembling, its stone walls cracking and crumbling in a dusty haze.

The ravens did not look back as the White Tower fell. They flew west over the Thames, the other ravens following with the magpies, jays, rooks and crows behind them in a formation as wide as the river and almost as deep. The water below them seemed alive with the reflection of the birds in flight.

They flew past *HMS Belfast*, over London Bridge, past the Monument and over Southwark Bridge.

One for sorrow, two for mirth...

Over Blackfriars Bridge, past Tate Modern, the Oxo Tower and Gabriel's Wharf, the black convoy cast a menacing shadow over the river. After Hungerford Bridge, the six ravens in front changed their course, turning north from the river by the London Eye. Some of the crows on the outer edge of the formation smashed into the glass pods, killing themselves and injuring almost a hundred tourists who had been hoping for a bird's-eye view of the celebrations on The Mall.

Three for a wedding...

Over Westminster Bridge they flew, over the Houses of Parliament, where they skimmed the hands of Big Ben as they began their descent.

Below them, hundreds of thousands of people were lining the streets on the north bank of the river. Young and old, local and foreign, reporters and paparazzi were pushing against the barriers for a better view of the procession to come. Scores of police were at hand to keep rowdier revellers back, but for the most part, the crowd was in good spirits.

The excited chatter soon gave way to gasps and cries as people started looking up. Expecting a cloud over the sun, they saw instead the blanket of birds overhead.

Thor, Mugin, Bran, Hugine, Branwen and Matthew circled Westminster Abbey, signalling to the others that they had arrived at their destination. The six ravens descended and landed on the sill of a stained-glass window depicting Abraham, Isaac, Jacob and fourteen prophets. The other birds followed, settling on every available perch until the abbey was covered in their jostling bodies.

Inside, the heir to the throne and his young bride were exchanging rings as the Royal Family proudly looked on. The King and his Princess Consort, the Duke of York, the Earl and Countess of Wessex, uncles, aunts, cousins and second cousins from all over the country and the continent; all were there to witness the royal nuptials.

As the congregation rose to the opening strains of Handel's Wedding March, Thor began to peck at the stained glass. *Tap. Tap. Tap.* The other birds joined in. Thousands of beaks pecked at every window, every door, every roof tile. *Tap-tap-tap-tap-tap.*

Crack.

A prophet's face shattered.

A waterman's tale

Tim Segaller

"Thirty-five years I've been working on the river. Must have done 10,000 trips in that time. It's been my life, the Thames has – I wouldn't be the man I am without it. And now they want to take all that away from me."

So Bill Masters tells me over a beer in the crowded National Film Theatre bar overlooking the majestic Thames, lit up by the late afternoon sun.

"Well, I'm not going to let it happen," he continues. "I've got plans . . ."

Bill owns and pilots one of the boats that take tourists up and down the river. His daily route is between Westminster and Tower Hill, where the river acts as a kind of alternative to the Tube's Circle Line: the two run parallel to each other.

Bill's swelling pride in his job made me curious to find out more about the watermen of the Thames. Their story, in fact, goes back some 500 years. Back then, they were some of the most important tradesmen in London. Before the advent of cars and trains, the Thames was *the* highway of London for both goods and passengers. And at a time when there was only one bridge over the river, London Bridge, everyone relied on the watermen to get from bank to bank.

With so much business around, they flourished. Some of the less scrupulous among them started overcharging passengers. So an Act of Parliament was brought in to protect the public from dodgy dealing, thereby creating the first form of licensed public transport in London.

Further Acts of Parliament introduced seven-year apprenticeships on the river (a practice that continues to this day, although the period has shrunk to five years). The Worshipful Company of Watermen and Lightermen was set up to train apprentices and protect the interests of men working on the river. Still today, all new apprentices enter into an agreement with the company and are bound to a master who is himself a licensed waterman. The master supervises the apprentice's training and finds work experience for him or her on every part of the tidal Thames, from Gravesend in Kent to Teddington in west London.

Like many watermen, Bill comes from a family that has worked on the Thames for generations. At just 15, he was apprenticed to his father, who had in his time been apprenticed to his father. "I always knew I'd follow the family way," he says. "I can still remember the first time I went on the river with my dad. It was down at Gravesend, where I grew up. It was cold and wet and we had a crappy old boat carrying coal. But I was so excited about my first job – my new life."

Two years later, already an experienced young waterman, Bill went for an oral exam at the Waterman's Hall behind Old Billingsgate Market. He had to stand in front of a panel of senior watermen seated at a long table in a wood-panelled room. He was too young and nervous to appreciate all the tradition and finery around him. But he answered every question put to him on the 98 miles of the tidal Thames correctly, and gained his provisional licence.

He served out the remaining five years of his apprenticeship and received his full licence and the freedom of the river. And he carried on working for his father, who was more of a lighterman (carrying cargo) than a waterman (carrying passengers), for another 14 years. "Dad was always much happier dealing with sacks of coal than people," he recalls. "They would never ask you stupid questions, he used to say. That's where we're different. I love dealing with people, even the tourists who ask stupid questions."

When his father retired, Bill took out a bank loan to set up a business offering tourist trips along the river. It was an inspired decision: word spread and the tourists kept on coming. At first he simply took them down the river pointing out various sites along the way while they looked at their maps. Then he had a bright idea for an added feature to draw in the crowds: providing a running commentary over a loudspeaker on places of historical interest along the route. The tourists loved it, and told him so. His commentaries, he boasts, have become almost legendary among his fellow watermen.

I ask him for a flavour of his spiel, and he obliges. "One of my favourites is about St Paul's. First I tell them that it was built by Sir Christopher Wren, stands at 365 feet and boasts the second-largest unsupported dome in the world. I explain that Wren designed 52 churches and public buildings, only a couple of dozen of which survive today, and that there isn't a single statue or picture of him in any of them. But on his tomb in St Paul's itself, there is a brass plaque that reads: 'I told you I was ill.' OK, it's hardly the funniest gag ever. Not in the best taste, either. But they laugh every time – guaranteed."

There's a brief silence as we sip our beer and smile over the joke. Then I ask him how he sees business on the river in the future, and gloom descends. I probe further; it turns out that things aren't looking good for the Thames watermen. A new EU Boatmaster's Licence is to entitle anyone in the EU to work on the Thames after an apprenticeship of just two years, as opposed to the mandatory five years that a Thames waterman must serve.

"Two years to get to know the Thames properly? They must be having a laugh!" Bill rages. "The river can be very hard to navigate, especially round the piers and pontoons. It's all about local knowledge. That's exactly why they brought in licences all those centuries ago, to stop the terrible accidents that inexperienced watermen had. And now they want to take us back to those days. I mean, can you imagine it: some 18-year-old kid who's spent a couple of summers taking a piddling little boat up the Seine or the Rhine or whatever, having to work close-quarter manoeuvres in the rapid tides of the Thames? Mark my words, there will be casualties – maybe even deaths. And I *will* say I told you so."

Bill feels that he and his fellow watermen have been badly let down by the Company of Watermen and Lightermen. He thinks they should have dismissed the new EU licence out of hand. Instead, they have said merely that they will make sure the new licence takes proper account of local knowledge. The problem, as he sees it, is that the 26 members of the company's governing body (known as the "Court") are out of touch with the reality of life on the Thames for watermen today. He complains that some of them don't even qualify to be Journeymen Freemen of the company under the 1859 Watermen's Act. In other words, they aren't allowed to pilot a boat down the Thames. They are known instead as Craft-owning Freemen, which means they buy their Freedom of the Company. "It feels as though – and pardon the play on words – we're being sold down the river."

Some of the watermen have joined a breakaway group, the River Thames Watermen's and Lightermen's Association, to challenge the new legislation and the dominance of the Waterman's Hall. Bill has considered joining the new group, but feels nothing can stop the new licence from taking effect and putting dozens of watermen out of business. "We've seen it all before," he laments. "Valiant attempts to beat the Brussels bureaucrats. You remember the metric martyr? He put up a damn good fight, but he just couldn't buck the system, could he?"

The gloom deepens as Bill tells me that his son Jim has recently decided against serving a waterman's apprenticeship in favour of a more lucrative and secure career in IT. But then his spirits revive as he explains that there should be enough custom from tourists on the river to last him until he retires. In fact, Bill clearly has a good business head. If the work does dry up, he plans to diversify by setting up a training school for people applying for the new European Boatmaster's Licence.

"Some of my fellow watermen would probably say I'm just selling out. I guess they may have a point. And I know full well that my new venture won't be the same as mastering an apprentice in the traditional Thames way. But times change and you have to change with them. That's just the way of things."

Bill Masters is fictional; the issues raised in this piece are not.

MONUMENT

Monumoments

Lessons in life that Monument has taught me
by Neil Taylor, aged 28 ½

A Saturday in spring: **You're never as fit as you used to be.**
It's hard to breathe. I'm panting out shallow wheezy gasps, the
air forced to corkscrew through my constricting throat as my
clambering, stumbling frame corkscrews its way to the top of the
column. Some have fallen by the wayside, biding their time in
asthmatic alcoves. Small children are getting jittery limbs. There's
the odd bout of vertigo as people look down the spiral staircase.
And down, and round, and down.

Today: **Don't miss the obvious.**

There is a monument at Monument. Not a lot of people know that.

Perpendicular to the Circle Line Tube is another tube: *the* monument. A great column. But you could walk past it (or be whisked off beneath it) and never know it was there. It's been hemmed in, lost to the sky. Like the London Eye, it can be so far out of kilter with its neighbours that it disappears. But it's there. Occasionally you catch a glimpse of the golden ball of flame atop it reflected in the glass wall or smoked window of a City office block. Yes, the suits ignore it. It is known only to panting children and German tourists, leaving their mark in bright pink felt-tip. Fire was here.

2 *September 1666:* **Look for what's hidden.**

The Monument was designed to commemorate the Great Fire of London. Not London's only great fire, but the one we know best. The word "monument" comes from a Latin one about warnings. So that's what it is. A tall Doric fire alarm designed by Christopher Wren.

But not just that. Between the tower and the Tube, there's a laboratory where Robert Hooke made investigations of enormous gravity (namely the Earth's). When people climb to survey London, razed by flame then raised again, they become gremlins, impurities, ghosts in the machine. The machine we mount is a sometime telescope and housing for a pendulum.

2 *September 1667:* **Learn from your mistakes.**

So I make it to the top, look around and across. The Monument has a few like-minded friends: the top of St Paul's, Nelson and his column. But it's being crowded out of the skyline by curves of glass, gherkins, looming canaries. Shrinking as the City clambers upwards. Ideas above its station.

Look down, and not much has changed. Eastcheap sweeps, and Bishopsgate trundles north. The streets laid waste in 1666 grew back like eucalyptus after a bush fire. It wasn't to Wren's taste. He mapped out new New World grids, Parisian groves and boulevards. But before his draughtsman's ink was dry, London was back. The same streets on the same routes, ringing with the same tunes. The memory of the flames leaping from roof to roof across narrow lanes meant nothing. Londoners built exactly where they'd built before, and the streets came back defiant, stubborn, narrow and flammable as ever.

August 1850: **Entropy.**

I'm not a scientist, but I've always liked the idea of entropy, or at least the version that got talked about in *Doctor Who*: that one of the laws of the universe is "the more you put things together, the more they fall apart." The glass half-empty version of this means there's no point trying to make anything better. I prefer the glass half-full version: that life has a natural equilibrium. Constrain it in one way and it will burst out in another.

In the fire, 13,200 houses were destroyed, and 87 churches: 346 acres of destruction. A seventeenth-century Ground Zero. Yet reputedly, miraculously, only six people died. The Monument rose, yet more people fell. For in time another seven people threw themselves from its top onto the cobbles below. Entropy.

The top is now encaged: no jumping, no diving, no bombing (that's why these days they search your bags).

Monday morning, 8.52: **Go with the flow from time to time.**

Or, as Sendrine would say, "Today I disguise myself as ant." These days in EC3, you are not you. You are an insect in a suit of black or grey.

You may believe you still exist – through a flash of studiedly individual tie, or the random flare of a fluorescent jacket lining – but you have lost. You will be channelled. You will be channelled through the white tile lanes between Bank and Monument. You will be channelled across London Bridge in emergent columns of back and forth. You will be channelled up the tower in dizzying, wearying single file. Like the streets that grew back where they were before, this is where human will is weak. The city is in charge.

1677: **Look for patterns.**

The Monument is 202 feet tall, and 202 feet from the smouldering oven in the baker's shop in Pudding Lane where the Great Fire started. Christopher Wren was an architect with faith in the power of the stories numbers tell (like Daniel Libeskind, whose Freedom Tower at Ground Zero in New York will be 1,776 feet tall, for the year of American independence).

13 April 2005: **Don't believe everything you're told.**
We're in the control room of the station, Sendrine and I, and the
clocks are going backwards. People are called, and badgered to
bring ladders. The Monument's in scaffolding. Tourists arrive
perplexed; they're told it's being moved four feet, or it's Nelson.
They believe. "It's a wonder they ever get here in the first place,"
someone says.

3 September 1666: **Don't be greedy.**
Some, when they weren't blaming the Catholics, put the fire
down to gluttony or greed (forgive me, I am unsubtle and can
never remember the difference). In 1681 they added to the
inscription on the side of the Monument to blame the fire on a
"Popish frenzy." By 1831 the Catholics were no longer the bad
guys, and it got scratched out again.

Were Londoners so greedy then? Well, the fire started in Pudding and ended in Toast, spreading through Fish Street Hill and
Poultry. But it seems we really do never learn. Now you reach the
bottom only to be seduced by Treats and Snax, berry scones and
chocolate-chunk cookies.

Saturday morning, 8.52: **Remember to take a break.**
A van passes that says "This is London." That's right. This is
where the city, and the City, started. From AD 43 to EC3, two
millennia of London life have wheeled and dealed and wailed
and sailed past Monument. That's why this is *London* Bridge and
the others aren't.

But the City is like a word whose meaning has narrowed. A
"knight" used to be any old sort, not necessarily one of chivalry
and valour. "Meat" used to mean any kind of food. And a
"budget" was just a little bag for keeping things in. The City of
London was always made for trade, but it had more: churchgoers,
players, protesters, prostitutes . . . residents. Now, like the budget,
the City's meaning is married to money, and not much more.
Monday to Friday, nine to five, the black, the red, insure, re-
insure, credit, debit, buy, sell. Sell, sell, sell.

So visit Monument Tube on a weekend and listen to the sound
of your own footsteps echo through its deserted chambers. It's a
piece of land that's found two days of peace and quiet. It is semi-
retired, hustled and bustled into submission and out of life. OK,

OK, enough already; gimme a break. So now we do. Saturdays and Sundays, this is no man's land. The City becomes its own monument.

18 April 1913: Stand up for what you believe in.
In 1913, two suffragettes took the Monument, all out for death or victory, and the authorities could break back in only with a "lustily wielded sledgehammer," said *The Times*. But the crowd outside were lusty too. The police took the two back into the Monument to save them from the assembled throng. And only the Tube could save them: they were escorted away through Monument station while the masses massed.

Friday lunchtime: Take a walk on the wild side.

These days, Monument is border country. To the north there are banks and bankers, corneys and barrows, slugs and lettuces and many a starbuck. The south is another country. You can see them – the insects in suits – making safe passage across the bridge between the hours of eight and nine. And again, between six and seven, when they fly south for the night. They avoid the tramps of London Bridge station. Some might chance a glance among the rare breeds and organic herbs of Borough Market, but not for long. They sidestep the patients of the Weston Unit and smirk contempt at the jobbing actors of the London Dungeon (don't worry, the blood that flows in the dark is only water).

Today: Things aren't as simple as they seem.
Look at the Tube map: Monument, Bank. Bank, Monument. Graphically, they are married, bound together, thick as thieves, close as close can be. But listen, tourist: it is treachery.

The walk between Monument and Bank stations takes an age. They're not married; they are separated and edging towards divorce. Their union is a theoretical one, the sleight of a cartographer's hand. Yes, yes, London Underground will tell you it's one station. A complex. A hub. Ring Monument station and they answer, "Hello, Bank." Nonsense; they are worlds apart.

(Queensway and Bayswater: now *they're* close. There too the map will deceive you: it refuses to admit their affair. But we know.)

CANNON STREET

No cannons

As told to Dan Germain

Wandering around. That's what I was best at. Had a home but that was a while ago. In a place called Roade. Figures. Born in Roade, live on a road, sort of king of the road. But I wouldn't call myself a king. Don't see many kings in my game. Had a mug once with a picture of the king on it. Don't know where that went.

Being on the road, you sometimes get asked what it's like. Quite a lot of the time you don't get asked though. People don't tend to stop and talk much. Had a fella who always liked to stop and talk but he doesn't come past any more. We used to talk about the news. I like to keep up with the news. It's good to know about the world. In India they have blokes like me who wander around but they get a lot more respect over there. Holy men, like vicars or priests but with long beards. Some of them crawl from place to place. Never walk. Just crawling all the time, like a punishment for the bad stuff they might do later. Get it in the bank. Get ready for the bad times by saying sorry first. Quite clever, that is.

Anyway, that fella who used to stop. He was always curious about the road. I said to him that you can't just decide to be on the road. There's more to it than that. You've got to try other stuff first. I tried being in a house but was never into it. Ended up sleeping out the back in the garden for a while. Who says you've got to live in a house? Far as I can see the world is a big old place and there's a lot of room. Plenty of room for a man to sleep outside. You can build a house if you want but then you're stuck. Same place every day. Get up in the morning and look out of the window. Same view. Same other house across the street, same silver car, same dog yapping. What's the point of that? You want to look at the same thing every day? Fair enough when things get a bit worse, like me now with my leg. You might have to calm down a bit. Might not be able to run around as much. But when you're young.

You should get out, that's what I said to the fella. Why do you come up and down here every day? Why do you get on that train? He laughed most of the time. Said he'd love to jack it in but his missus would kill him, and then we'd talk about women and how life was different when you had to look after them. Not that I'd know much about that, but I could see his point. Came every day from Dartford and had to work to make sure his missus was happy and that he could pay the rent. Used to say I was lucky not to have a missus and rent and all that. Said that I could just wander off and find somewhere new. I told him I was done with all that, with the leg and everything. He asked me why I chose this spot if I could wander off and have any spot in the world. And I have to admit that I'd lie to him 'cos I don't know why I ended up here. No one reason in particular.

After all the things I've seen. To end up down here.

The road from Roade. I like saying that. If I was a writer that'd be the name of my book. The road from Roade. I think it's the A five-oh-something. Doesn't matter. The road from Roade is the thing. I went down it and never went back. There's an interesting thing. Never went back to Roade. No real reason to, 'cos I'd seen it. Seen the houses, met some people, had some teachers and got bored of the bus and the garage. Wasn't anything left to see in Roade so I went and left.

And after that I went everywhere. Been to Scotland. Been to Wales. Been to Canterbury and then Dover, and even went to France. France wasn't all that. Same cars, same kind of people. Weather was the same and when I went to the countryside, that was the same too. So I came back. Went to Bournemouth. Liked Bournemouth but had to leave. Went to Cornwall for the summer but after that things weren't good. Didn't go anywhere for a while. Not really my fault. They just said I couldn't go anywhere. For my own good. I told them that if they wanted to do me some good, they'd let me get back to the road.

That was a while down there. Long old time. Then I got back on the road. A relief. Slept everywhere else for a long old time. In fact, that's when I started a project. Tried to sleep in a different place every night. A bit like those Indian vicars I was going on about. A holy man trying to see everywhere but not being anywhere. That's what they say about God. He's everywhere but he isn't anywhere. Don't get me wrong. I didn't think I was God. I've had my problems but I'm not that daft. Just wanted to get about and challenge myself a bit. Didn't want to get like the other ones I met. Stuck in the same spot, always moaning and begging and making a nuisance. Give me a bad name, that lot.

Then I got down here. It's warmer than wandering all the time. At my age you have to think about staying warm. That's how I ended up with a spot if I'm being honest. Staying warm. To be honest, the proper wandering is a young man's game. I'm still trim but I ain't young and the leg bothers me enough to stay put these days. That young fella, the one who used to stop and talk, he'd ask about the leg but I told him that it was none of his business. Polite and everything, but it was none of his business. If he wanted to talk about wandering and the life, I'd say that was fine and we'd have a talk. But the leg is my business.

He said to me once that I should write it all down. I told him about the road from Roade, and he said he thought it'd be good. He said that all you read these days is books about spies and murders and that my book would be totally original. That's his words. Totally original. Not made up like most of the books. He reckoned I knew more than any of that lot. Than any of the lot on his train. But he stopped coming through. A real shame, that. He was ever so nice, polite. I hope him and his missus are all right down in Dartford. Don't know how it would have worked though. Writing it all down. I'm not that good with the writing. Talking's fine. He could have done it, the writing. But like I said, he's not about any more.

So it's all here. The only thing they haven't got is cannons. They do, you know, they reckon there are big old cannons down here. Come out with their maps and bags and ask someone where the cannons are. Never ask me, which is stupid 'cos I'm here most of the time. If there were some cannons I'd know about it. Funny thing is I don't get that bored. I've seen some things. Seen Stonehenge. Seen the sea in a few different places. Seen the White Cliffs of Dover. Stayed down there for a while after France. They all looked nicer than round here. I always said that if I had to have a spot it'd be time to shoot me. Snap my neck.

But I just got a bit stuck and stayed here and got fed up of the wandering if the truth be told. And it's not too bad. To be honest, enough was enough. I reckon even those Indian fellas must have to stop one day, just find a spot and sit down. All that crawling. Nice to have it in the bank but you don't want to be crawling too long.

Tracks of time

Simon Jones

The old man is moving without effort. He glides through a white underground passage, watching people pass the other way on the iron escalator. He searches their faces with interest but gets nothing in return. They stare straight ahead with the same blank expression, seemingly oblivious to the adverts pushing self-tan, mobile phones and multivitamins. It's as though they are lost in a single thought.

The handrail judders and he shuffles forward from escalator to floor. But now he moves slowly, and the crowds behind him suddenly wake from their dream. They surge for the exit, brushing him aside as they go.

"I've used this station all my life," he grumbles, "and I've never known such rudeness. Where are people's manners these days?"

Toddy mumbles like this every day, but no one hears him any more. Sometimes he feels as though he no longer exists. And the insistent pain in his hip makes him wonder if one day he'll be too old to make this journey. Will the small step from the escalator become too much? Will he lose the freedom of his city?

He leaves the station and walks along the busy city street. It's hot outside. Businessmen rush past with sweat soaking into their pristine white collars. The cycle couriers move more slowly than usual. Toddy squints against the light, cursing the modern glass façades that reflect the light so harshly. They seem crudely at odds with the warm glow of old stone buildings that crowd into the same streets. But this area is full of contrasts, from the pure white tower of St Mary to the dour concrete slabs of 1960s office blocks. This is Mansion House. A cauldron of architecture, people and history. A place Toddy loved from the day he arrived.

He moved to London from Rotherham when he was twenty-one. Having found work tending the gardens of Regent's Park, he felt as though he was making a life for himself. He chose to live in Mansion House because he couldn't imagine anything grander than passing the Lord Mayor of London's residence every time he walked to the Tube. And although he hasn't always approved of the way the area has changed over the years, with the rise of pompous eateries and cheap sandwich bars with no seats, he still feels he belongs. He always thinks banks and business make the area feel like the root of civilised life, the height of human achievement.

Walking home in the heat, Toddy hears a friendly voice calling him over and is glad of the excuse to stop.

"Morning to you there, Toddy. Fine day again. Blue skies all over."

Toddy turns to see an old face peering back at him from behind a tiny booth stacked high with the morning's papers, cigarettes, crisps, sweets and his pet hate, chewing-gum.

"I don't know why you insist on selling this rubbish, Jack," Toddy says, half-smiling. "It's all over the streets and if it's not getting on your shoes you find it stuck to your arse."

"Good for the breath, my friend. And in my job, I need to stay fresh as a daisy. Never know who you might meet in this line of work."

It has been their routine for the past fifteen years, but it never fails to make both men laugh. Although Jack is a little younger than Toddy, he is a stubborn smoker and breaks into a cough.

"What do they say today?" Toddy asks, nodding at the papers.

"Another politician caught in embarrassing circumstances," Jack says, "one from the other side this time. That makes it about thirty all, by my reckoning. Can't see what any young lady would see in him, though. Face like a smacked badger. Must be a power thing.

"And you'll like this one, my friend. Plans for another of them hyper-modern office buildings. All glass and metal, and almost as big as that gherkin thing over there. Going up on the other side of town. Wonder how much they'll spend on it?"

"What's this one called, the turnip?" Toddy says. "Ridiculous, the whole thing. As if there weren't enough buildings around here. They used to make things to last. Look at Mansion House. As fine today as the day it was built. And it doesn't need a military operation to clean its windows every time a pigeon does its business. We need people with a bit of sense."

Noticing his annoyance, Jack tries to change the subject, but Toddy is no longer listening.

"And manners. You know what happened to me today? This hooligan thundered past me in the Tube. No thought. Bashed me with his shoulder and sent me flying into the wall. Oh, did I get angry. 'Careful!' I said. 'You carry on like that and you'll have me to deal with.'"

"Toddy?"

"I should have got him by his ear and took him home to his mother. No discipline, these kids. Spitting everywhere and daubing obscenities on every surface in the city. Well, I've got a few obscenities of my own for them . . ."

"Toddy?" Jack says. "The usual?"

"Ay?"

"The *Mail*?"

"Yeah, and a pack of them mints," Toddy replies, checking his temper. "You never know who I might meet."

−O−

It's such a warm day that Toddy can't stay in his dingy flat. So, leaving his jacket, jumper and even his tie hanging in the wardrobe, he takes the Tube to Regent's Park. It's particularly beautiful at this time of year, he thinks. The yellow and white of early spring flowers have given way to deeper, more mature colours. Toddy stops by a clump of bluebells nestling in the shade of a tall hedge. He's watched this little community grow and fade every year since he started work at the park, and likes to check on their progress, raising the heads gently with his fingertips to look inside.

He's surprised at the heat as he wanders, trailing his hand along the hedge like a child. The weather has lifted London's spirits. Sunbathing couples lie exposing their pallid skin just yards from the path. Boys and girls and boys and boys and girls and girls entwined. Toddy draws breath through his nose and keeps his eyes on the path. Every year they get more risqué, wear fewer clothes and embrace one another more openly. Don't any of them have jobs? Two o'clock on a weekday afternoon and the park is full of lounging bodies. Such indolence would not have been tolerated when Toddy was young.

He stops for a moment to wipe the sweat from his neck with a handkerchief. Is the world getting hotter? Global warming because of all the cars? He's seen documentaries on TV and needs no persuading.

"Parents don't walk their children to school any more; they just drive ridiculous off-road jeeps through choking city streets. It's just laziness, like couples dozing in the park on a Wednesday afternoon."

He catches himself mumbling again. What was he saying? He knows he has a point. But as he traces his thoughts, the sounds of the park merge into a hazy, far-off hum, making his mind misty and tired.

Then he sees it, lying on the ground. The remnants of a packed lunch: Coke can, sandwich wrapper, crisp packet. Despite the stiffness in his back and knees he bends down and plucks the items from the ground, scratching his nails through the earth.

Graham Stead is in his early forties, with pale receding hair and a permanently sceptical expression. He's been a gardener at Regent's Park for two years.

"What's this?" Toddy says as he approaches. Stead, who is stooped behind a park bench tending a fern with tiny secateurs, rises and turns. He looks at Toddy's muddy outstretched hand and clutch of litter.

"Rubbish," says Stead.

"And do you know where I got it?"

"How are you today, Toddy?" he says, smiling at the old man.

"Standards are slipping. I've talked to you about this before. I just can't turn a blind eye to this."

"And nor should you. But even with all the best efforts of the people who work here, we can't be right behind every thought-less kid that chucks their wrappers on the ground. When we see it, we pick it up. Drives me crazy as well."

"Well, you should be more diligent. Kids lazing all over the place, dropping rubbish, no thought or care . . ."

Toddy trails off mid-sentence. He knows he's talking to the wrong person; it would be impossible to keep the park free of rubbish even with a team of thousands. He feels so powerless to do anything about it. If he's honest, there was always rubbish scattered about when he worked here too, but he doesn't want to remember that. He finds himself short of words, and the weather seems to be closing in on him. He steadies himself with a hand on the back of the bench.

"You OK?" Stead asks, reaching out to him.

"Yes, yes. I'm fine. Just going to have a little rest here. Leave me be."

Stead waits for a moment while the old man sits down. Then, satisfied he's OK, he wanders off to finish his tasks in time to enjoy the evening sun and a beer.

Toddy sits rigidly for a few moments, his hands gripping the edge of the bench. Images of the park swim before his eyes, merging into a gaudy blur. Sounds become distant. He has a vague memory: the feeling of his body in easy motion, walking through a white tunnel. Mansion House? Is he back on the station platform waiting for a train to take him to work? Tools by his side, giving him a sense of purpose and belonging? Through the air comes the snip-snip of busy shears and the muffled crunch of a trowel digging earth. But he is still in the tunnel, and a shiver of happiness surges through his youthful body. The sounds whirling round him intensify; the rails rattle and wind blasts across the platform. They continue to rise, flooding his ears, until they are almost too much to bear. Then suddenly they begin to fade, like a train moving into the distance, until Toddy hears no more.

–O–

For a moment, the sharp white light convinces Toddy he is back in Mansion House. He breathes a deep, happy sigh. But as he blinks, the room takes shape and he feels crisp white sheets pulled close under his chin. A nurse is standing at the end of his bed. She turns round when she hears him moan.

"Morning, Mr Johnson, how are you today?"

"What happened?" Toddy says.

"You had a bit of a funny turn in the park. Nothing to worry about. You slipped off a bench and banged your head."

"Am I going to be all right?"

"Yes, you're fine. We've run a couple of tests and just need to keep you in for a day or so, that's all. Maybe you've been overdoing it a bit recently?"

"How did I get here?"

"The young man you were with in the park called an ambulance. He insisted on following to the hospital to see if you were OK."

"Graham?" asks Toddy.

"No, I think his name was Jack. He came back earlier to check on you and said he'll help you home tomorrow. How do you know him?"

–O–

Toddy meets young Jack the next day as they walk to a cab outside the hospital. Jack has shoulder-length hair and metal in his nose. With chewing gum shoved to one side of his mouth, he says he's a programmer living in Camden, and a keen jogger. He recognised Toddy from the park, and was first on the scene when he passed out. He insists on seeing the old man safely home. Jack has an open face; an innocence that makes Toddy feel he can trust him.

In the cab, the two gaze silently through the window until Toddy says, "My friend's called Jack too. He runs a little news-stand near my home."

"Cool. If you want, we could stop off and grab a paper. What do you read?" Jack says.

"Why are you doing all this?" Toddy asks. "Calling an ambulance for a stranger in the park is one thing, but why all the concern? I'm grateful to you, but I don't understand why you care."

The two men stare at each other for a long time. Toddy wonders what he is thinking. What makes a young man interested in someone so old? Then Jack slowly says, "Not enough people care these days. What does it cost me? A bit of time, that's all. No big deal, old man. Anyway, you remind me of my grandad."

Toddy rests his head against the seat and lets his shoulders relax. He hasn't taken a cab through London for a long time; it feels like a rare luxury to watch all the buildings pass by. These narrow streets and grand towers must hold the key to so many secrets. Stories like his own, perhaps, that start out with so much energy and then gradually fade away. If he tried, could he make Jack understand his life? Could he paint a picture of so many years in just a few moments?

They drive past Mansion House station and Toddy asks the driver to stop. He can walk home from here, where every brick holds a memory, every doorway is a link to another time. Toddy opens the cab door and turns to his young friend.

"Could I trouble you for a piece of gum?" he says.

BLACKFRIARS

Holy shit

How to get out of Blackfriars

Nick Asbury

Exit 5: What's the point?
Blackfriars is a miserable, misshapen, browbeaten sort of place.
More or less everything about it has been messed up in some
way. Pillars stand sheepishly in the Thames, bereft of a bridge to
support. Landmarks of breathtaking historical importance are
torn down, only to reappear thousands of miles away. Stations
hop across the river, realise their mistake and hop back again.
Once noble holy men become fodder for theme pubs. Rivers
stagnate into open sewers, disappear underground and bubble
up unexpectedly, spewing excrement all over the place.

*Directions: On exiting the barriers, make your way down the maze
of tunnels towards Exit 5. Lose heart halfway, retrace your steps
and consider going to Temple instead.*

Exit 1: You'll feel better after a beer

Blackfriars takes its name from the black-robed Dominican friars who once held a grand monastic estate here. Their mission was to provide much-needed practical support and spiritual sustenance to the City's labouring classes and thousands of malnourished poor. Today, their influence lives on in the names of several decent bars and restaurants, including: the 11th Commandment (platters, cocktails, candles); the Evangelist (Modern European, pricey); and the Black Friar itself. This incongruous wedge-shaped pub looks like it got off the Tube at the wrong stop and decided to stick around anyway. It used to be an office block, but was expensively converted in 1905 by the architect H. Fuller Clarke. He called in the Royal Academy sculptor Henry Poole to create the exterior's ornate façade, along with its marbled walls, pillared fireplaces and bas-reliefs of monks playing out various scenes accompanied by tangentially apposite mottos: *Wisdom is rare, Finery is foolery, Don't advertise, tell a gossip* and so on. Somewhat unfairly, the Black Friar has been described as the nation's first-ever theme pub, but it remains a singular example of urban Arts and Crafts at its best. The only problem is that it has occasionally been known to smell a bit.

Directions: Head straight up the steps at Exit 1 and follow your nose.

Exit 6: An interesting drain cover

Blackfriars is a river mouth. It's where the Fleet meets the Thames, having flowed all the way down from Hampstead, through Kentish Town and St Pancras, round Clerkenwell Hill and under Holborn Bridge. Although shallow, the river was once wide enough to accommodate a fair amount of shipping; a rusty anchor was found as far north as Kentish Town. However, by the sixteenth century it had become almost completely clogged up with rubbish and raw sewage. Increasingly desperate attempts to clean it invariably met with failure. Sir Christopher Wren got involved at one point, and the lower part of the river was widened into a canal, while the section north of Holborn to the City wall was covered over. Unfortunately, the new canal still acted as a sewage-magnet, and the stench became steadily more noxious.

In 1732, the authorities admitted defeat and bricked the whole thing over from Holborn Bridge to Fleet Street, and later from

Fleet Street down to the Thames. But the river fought back. In 1846, it burst out of its brick casing and engulfed the streets above in a tidal wave of raw sewage. A steamboat was crushed against Blackfriars Bridge. Even today, building works along the course of the river have to be pumped out regularly, and the waters can flood the roadway in severe storms. All this may well have something to do with the funny smell in the Black Friar.

Directions: As you come out by the river, follow the walkway beneath the road bridge. Under the first arch, when the water is low enough, you can see a large metal drain cover. It's the only remaining sign of where the Fleet flows into the Thames.

Exit 2: Pursued by a bear

Blackfriars is actually quite a likeable place. Just a short stroll north of the station lies Playhouse Yard. This is where the Blackfriars Playhouse used to stand, the theatre in which several of Shakespeare's greatest plays were first performed. In cultural importance, it's perhaps second only to the Globe, on the other side of the river. But is there a reconstruction of the Blackfriars Playhouse? No. Maybe a visitor centre? No again. Surely a plaque of some sort? Well, best not to make a fuss about it.

Carry on walking towards Ireland Yard and you'll see the Cockpit Tavern, site of the gatehouse that Shakespeare bought in 1612. This is one of the few solid facts that we know about Shakespeare's life. His signature is on the deeds. But again, nothing to mark the spot, not so much as a plaque. Blackfriars wears its history lightly, with a casual shrug. There's something heart-warming about it.

Directions: Head straight on under the bridge, across Queen Victoria Street, up Blackfriars Lane, and Playhouse Yard is on your right. Facilities include a circular bench with some shrubs in the middle.

Exit 9: Staunton, Virginia, USA

As it turns out, the Americans are already doing the Shakespeare heritage job for us. If you're ever passing through the town of Staunton, Virginia, you'll see signs everywhere pointing you towards the Blackfriars Playhouse. The theatre was built in 2001 as a faithful replica of the one that once stood in London EC4.

They're even planning to build their own version of the Globe next door. It's tempting to build a replica of Staunton City Hall in Playhouse Yard, just to even things up a bit.

Directions: Exit 9 is next to the main ticket office in the overground station. Ignore it and take the Thameslink northbound to Gatwick instead. Book yourself on the next flight to Philadelphia, then catch a short connecting flight to Shenandoah Regional Valley Airport in Virginia. Take a cab to Staunton and ask for the Blackfriars Playhouse on South Market Street.

Exit 8: Lonely, lacklustre and laughable

Shakespeare would often have made the walk from Blackfriars to St Paul's to browse its thriving bookstalls. In 1604, he might even have flicked through a copy of *A Table Alphabeticall*, the first-ever all-English dictionary, compiled by Robert Cawdrey and sold at the north door of St Paul's. The dictionary had only 2,500 entries and Shakespeare probably wouldn't have been impressed. Scholars have worked out that his vocabulary stretched to about 30,000 words, twice that of most educated people today. To be fair, he did make a lot of them up. Advertising, besmirch, elbow, hobnob, lonely, lacklustre and laughable all entered the language somewhere in the vicinity of Blackfriars. In fact, the area has reasonable grounds to call itself the linguistic and literary capital of London.

In 1755, Dr Johnson published his *Dictionary of the English Language*, the result of nine years' painstaking work at his house in Gough Square, just half a mile or so north of Blackfriars station. Samuel Pepys was born over the road in Salisbury Court. John Milton had lodgings in St Bride's churchyard, and probably saw a few plays at Blackfriars Playhouse before it closed in 1642 and was eventually demolished in 1655. St Bride's Church is the spiritual home of British journalism, a connection that can be traced all the way back to 1501, when William Caxton's assistant, the brilliantly named Wynkyn de Worde, set up England's first moveable-type press in the churchyard.

Directions: Straight up the main road, left at Bride Lane, left again at Fleet Street, right at Bolt Court and up into Gough Square; retrace your steps to Fleet Street, down through Salisbury Court and back towards Blackfriars, then along Queen Victoria Street and left up Godliman Street to St Paul's. Shakespeare also coined the term "wild-goose chase."

Exit 7: Some scaffolding

With all that sewage swilling about beneath Blackfriars, it's reassuring to know there's a local company dedicated to supplying us with products like Cif and Domestos. Unilever House is pretty spectacular as corporate headquarters go, its sweeping art deco exterior lending a welcome air of grandeur to an area somewhat in need of it. At the time of writing, the building is undergoing a two-year facelift, so there's not a lot to see. But there is talk of including some sort of public gallery in the revamped interior, so it may soon be possible to have a good nose around. Public access would be in keeping with a place where business and the arts have maintained an ambivalent but generally healthy relationship. Unilever is also the sponsor of the Unilever Series at Tate Modern, itself a good example of the arts flourishing in the spaces industry leaves behind.

Directions: As you come out of Exit 7, you'll see Unilever House straight ahead of you – or at least you will when they take the scaffolding down.

Exit 3: A bridge abridged

The two and a half bridges of Blackfriars have a complicated history. The road bridge was originally opened in 1769 during a great flurry of bridge building that marked the real birth of South London. (Until the eighteenth century, London Bridge was the only way of crossing the river.) Rebuilt a century later, the bridge now carries about 54,000 vehicles a day. In 1864, the first railway bridge came along, designed for the London, Chatham and Dover Railway Company and serving Blackfriars station, which opened in the same year and stood on the south bank. This is the bridge that has now become something of a folly. Unable to cope with the heavier modern trains, it fell into disrepair. Its fate was sealed when a bigger, brasher wrought-iron bridge opened in 1886: the one that is still in use today. With it came a new station on the north bank, originally called St Paul's. The south bank Blackfriars closed and eventually, in 1937, St Paul's stole its name.

If you go up to the overground station, you can still see a wall displaying the names of the stations served by the original Blackfriars, with destinations ranging from Margate to Marseille. A final twist: the situation is likely to get more confusing if the inauspiciously named Thameslink 2000 project ever gets off the ground. The plans include extending the platforms right across the river, with a new entrance on the south bank and glass awnings spanning the length of the bridge.

Directions: Head up the steps and out across the bridge. Gaze at the surreal rows of red pillars on your left, complete with the proud insignia of the London, Chatham and Dover Railway Company.

Exit 4: Final

Like most bridges in London, Blackfriars is one of those haunted places where many have come to take their own lives. Roberto Calvi may or may not have been one of them. Known as God's Banker for his links with the Vatican, he was the chairman of Banco Ambrosiano in Milan but became a central figure in a complex web of international fraud and intrigue. He had been missing for nine days when, in June 1982, a passer-by discovered his body hanging from scaffolding under the bridge, just above the riverside walkway. It was later revealed he had five bricks in his pockets, along with $15,000 in various currencies. An initial inquest verdict of suicide was overturned and the case remains unsolved, although four people were about to go on trial at the time of writing. Murmurs of Masonic links and Mafia connections have grown more insistent over the years.

Directions: Wander morbidly under the bridge where God's Banker met his end and ponder what the Dominican friars might have made of it all.

Exit 10: Holy shit

Blackfriars has its fair share of ghost stories. One concerns the church of St Andrew's-by-the-Wardrobe, which is one of the few stable points in the whole of Blackfriars; a church has stood on the site since the twelfth century. One of its three bells used to hang in the church of Avenbury in Herefordshire, and is said to ring of its own accord whenever a vicar of Avenbury dies. Round the back lies Wardrobe Place, once the site of the king's storeroom. Here, a lady dressed in white is said to drift aimlessly from door to door, although she is so timid that she disappears if you stare directly at her.

Finally, there's the Old Deanery in Dean's Court, once the residence of the Dean of St Paul's. It's said to be haunted by all manner of demons, although this was denied by the Very Reverend Martin Sullivan, who was Dean until 1977. He was sure the strange creaks and bumps that the rest of his family heard must have a rational explanation; probably something to do with the central heating. However, there was one thing that did bother him: his toilet-roll holder always used to go "decidedly wonky" whenever someone else was in the toilet, only to right itself again by the time he was called to fix it. He's reported to have said, "Since I can't conceive of a haunted toilet-roll holder, I can only put it down to my skill at do-it-yourself."

Perhaps he was right. Maybe the mysterious toilet-roll holder was merely a reminder of the fallibility of all human endeavour, rather than a conduit for supernatural forces. Nevertheless, there must have been times when this man of God sat in the smallest room of his Blackfriars home, reached for the toilet paper and wondered.

Directions: Exit 10 takes you out onto a concrete walkway that looks towards St Andrew's-by-the-Wardrobe. Don't take it – it's scary out there. Head back to the overground station and walk along the platform and out over the bridge. It's the best place to wait for a train in London, and not a bad way to get out of Blackfriars.

Temple of stories

Tim Rich

Pale light spills from the Tube entrance illuminating a still, silent figure in a monk's habit. A tip of nose protrudes from the raised hood.

Five people have introduced themselves to the man, given the password to confirm they've paid and assembled in an arc around him. The vole-like Melanie Westerhoff is brushing Jaffa Cake crumbs from the jumper of her monumental husband, Dieter. And the very beige and very waterproof Mikey and Peggy Timberlake from Oak Island, Nova Scotia are working hard to ignore their fifteen-year-old son, Drew, who is wearing a stained black T-shirt with "The Jesus and Mary Chain" emblazoned across the chest in red Gothic script.

The soft bongs of Ben carry six o'clock down the black Thames as a Bob Hoskins look-alike gruffs a straight path through home-bound commuters. He arrives in a waft of mothballs, and growls, "Nobby Moon from Battle. I've been told to say 'King Baldwin.'"

"Gather please," intones the monkish man, and his hood shoots back to reveal a bony face offering a smile. "Here begins our adventure, which you may have seen advertised in the leaflet as Ye Olde Hystorycal Gyyde's 30-Minute Da Vinci Code Walking Tour Experience, but which I prefer to call Circling the Temple of Stories with Crispin Gascoigne. I am Crispin Gascoigne."

The guests smile back, the zed of the *Gaz-* of Gascoigne zizzling in their ears. A pink bubble of gum balloons from Drew's mouth and bursts over his face.

"First, some historical notes from a writer," says Crispin. "Templar: Poor Knights of Christ and of the Temple of Solomon. A religious order of knighthood founded circa 1120 in Jerusalem by a group of French knights. The Templars were, with the Hospitallers, the most important military order of the Crusades. Accused of heresy and immorality by Philip IV of France, who feared their power, the Templars were suppressed by the papacy in 1312 with great cruelty.

"The site of the nearby law courts and Tube station was once owned by the Knights Templar. Their headquarters were near King Solomon's Temple in Jerusalem. They also called their headquarters in London and Paris Temple, hence the name of the station, which was opened on 30 May 1870.

"Not my lines but those of an unknown copywriter on behalf of London Underground," says Crispin. "Wonderful concision. Find the plaque by the station entrance and you can scribble it all down too." He claps violently, spins through 360 degrees – producing squeals and a fluorescent flash from his feet – then walks backwards onto the pavement of Victoria Embankment crying, "Come! Come! So much history, so little time!"

The group passes between the dragon statues marking the western boundary of the City and arrives at the Embankment gateway to Temple. "On our right and left are the Temple Gardens and all is dusky calm," says Crispin, "but in Shakespeare's *Henry V* this is where the dispute that leads to the Wars of the Roses is set, with each character indicating his allegiance by the colour of the rose he plucks from the bushes." Crispin throws open his arms and thesps, "'And here I prophesy this brawl today/Grown to this faction in the Temple garden/Shall send between the red rose and the white/A thousand souls to death and deadly night.'"

"*Henry VI*," booms Nobby, grinning.

"Pure invention by our friend Bill," says Crispin. "Never happened. Red and white roses are still planted here to commemorate the Wars, however. And now let us transcend into the numinous world of Temple," with which he strides beneath the arch of Sir Charles Barry's florid gatehouse, beckoning.

"This area is home to two of London's four Inns of Court, Inner Temple and Middle Temple," says Crispin, as he spirals along cobbled Middle Temple Lane. "The others are Gray's Inn and Lincoln's Inn. Every student barrister in Britain must belong to an Inn. The best students go on to shadow an experienced barrister – their pupillage – then compete for a tenancy in one of these chambers. See these lists of names by the doorways? They've made it to chambers, for now at least.

"I believe," continues Crispin, wiping a diamond of teardrop from each eye, "that barristers are the great storytellers of our age. Dramatist and actor, they use spoken words as a painter uses colour or a chef flavour. For clients, the barrister's narrative jousts can mean the difference between wealth and poverty, honour and shame, and, until quite recently, life and..." Crispin mimes a noose being pulled tight around his neck.

"Slipknot," says Drew, making a devil-horns sign with his left hand.

"Tutti. Allegro," sings Crispin, and he leads the bustling, rustling entourage into Crown Office Row, past Paper Buildings, then hard left through a tunnel into Church Court.

"Lo, the omphalos. Temple Church," says Crispin. And the group consumes a vision of the church in the milk-soft light of gas lamps and a fattening moon. "London's least appreciated treasure. Protected by these walls and passages. Temperamental opening times keep out vague enquirers. An unravished bride of quietness. The Round was built first, by the Knights Templar, and was consecrated in 1185 – that's more than 800 years ago.

"The circular design is an homage to the Church of the Holy Sepulchre in Jerusalem, and is a Templar architectural tradition," says Crispin, while smoothing the creases from his habit. "The chancel – the rectangular bit – was consecrated in 1240, and was built because feeble Henry III desired to be buried in the church. He later changed his mind, naturally.

"In the twelfth century this was an immensely powerful financial and diplomatic area. Pilgrims might bank their monies here and carry notes of credit redeemable at Templar centres abroad. A sort of medieval MasterCard affair. In fact, the entire domain was ruled by the Master of the Temple, and the priest here is still called the Master. Onward!"

The group bumble into the church, with Dieter hunched to avoid cracking skull on stone and Nobby singing "Non nobis domine non nobis" to the tune of the *Match of the Day* music. Crispin sweeps into the centre of the round nave, saying, "Here on the floor you can see the nine marble effigies of medieval knights. I am contractually obliged to tell you that they are mentioned in *The Da Vinci Cod*, and I do mean *Cod*. Look closely at the enigmatic positioning of their limbs. Clearly signifies something, but exactly what we do not know. That they were Crusaders? Perhaps. Just please don't mention the G word."

There's a whirl of raincoats and knapsacks as Peggy and Mikey twist to face Crispin. "G word?" they hiss.

"Grail," says Crispin. "Who needs a goose chase when we have such wonder all about? This nave is supported by these free-standing columns made of Purbeck marble – replacements put in after bombs damaged the church in, er..." He makes such an effort to avoid eye contact with Dieter that Dieter notices. "... In 1941. The walls and gallery of grotesque heads were originally painted in bold colours. Imagine the scene! The Templar knights would also exercise their guard lions here, walking them around the circle using very long, stiff leads made of Sussex oak."

"Lions on leads," says Drew. "Fucking A."

"If you have an ear for music you simply must visit on Sunday mornings," says Crispin. "Eleven fifteen a.m. Divine choir."

The group drifts around the church and out into the mint-fresh evening. "He reminds me of that Willy Wonka fella in the movie," says Mikey. "Gene Wilder in a monk suit," says Peggy. "Nope," says Mikey, "definitely Willy Wonka."

Melanie, on tiptoes, whispers into the ear of a crouching Dieter. He nods and approaches Crispin.

"My wife is confused by the lions," says Dieter, with a hint of a West Country accent. "She says they're not in her guidebook."

"There are no lions in her guidebook?" says Crispin.

"*Frobisher's Definitive London*," says Dieter.

"Ah, good old literal *Frobisher's*," says Crispin, sniffing. "It's a powerful image, isn't it? The knights in the Round, the leering gargoyles, the hidden treasury, those wild beasties."

"My wife thinks the lions bit didn't happen. Did it?" asks Dieter.

"Can you imagine it happening? It's a rather fabulous idea, isn't it?" says Crispin.

"Well, yes, but is it true?" says Dieter.

"Gosh," says Crispin, taking a step back and clutching at the plastic crucifix dangling from his neck. "Truth; now you're asking…"

"You made it up, didn't you?" says Dieter.

Crispin, standing on one leg, says, "Well, see it as a personal response to a mystical space, Dieter. An idea I wanted to share with your imagination. I like to add something to an area. I'm not able to say that it isn't true, nor that it is."

"And the rest, the other facts?" says Dieter.

"Oh, you'll find others think they're true," says Crispin, lightly hopping from one leg to the other, "because you'll find them in books. But all sorts of people write books these days. Personally, I never know whom to trust when it comes to history. If we're honest, our approach is enormously selfish, isn't it? We only remember what appeals to us. We rarely seek to join the dots between the stories we like. Seems like hard work. When was the last time you wrestled with a primary source of history? Wasn't it Nietzsche who said 'History is a combination of reality and lies. The reality of history becomes a lie. The unreality of the fable becomes the truth'?"

"Cocteau," shouts Nobby, walking into the shadows, cackling.

A plane moans overhead en route to City Airport. Crispin and Dieter stand in silence, looking beyond each other.

"Abandoned babies!" shrieks Crispin. "They were left here in the western doorway of the church in the hope that the members of the Inns would provide for them. They did, and every child took the surname Temple."

"Lamb of God," says Drew.

"*Et maintenant*," says Crispin, executing a pirouette. "My delight-ful pilgrims of pleasure, let us march further into the labyrinth."

The group stroll up and down Inner Temple Lane and Hare Court, the gas streetlamps chirruping like crickets. "On the right we see Dr Johnson's Buildings," says Crispin. "These chambers com-memorate the residence of Samuel Johnson here. His biographer, James Boswell, was a member of Inner Temple, by the way, as were Chaucer and Cowper; the Gilbert of Gilbert and Sullivan; the author of Dracula, Bram Stoker; and Mahatma Gandhi, the author of Indian self-rule. Prestissimo!"

And on they press, under flickering lamps, through tight passageways, along cobbled lanes. "And so we reach Middle Temple

Hall," says Crispin, "one of the most impressive dining halls in England. A hundred feet long. Students and barristers have gathered here since 1573. Round the walls are the shields of distinguished members including Thackeray, Dickens and Lord Tweedsmuir, better known as that prolific writer of fiction John Buchan. Yes, the author of *The Thirty-Nine Steps* was a tax-law specialist. Sir Francis Drake and Sir Walter Raleigh were members too. As was I."

Melanie and Dieter catch each other's eye.

"Just to our right you see the ancient mulberry trees of Fountain Court resting on their crutches," says Crispin. "In *The Pickwick Papers* Dickens describes his young characters' adventures by the pond: 'Brilliantly the Temple Fountain sparkled in the sun, and laughingly its liquid music played, and merrily the idle drops of water danced and danced, and, peeping out in sport among the trees, plunged lightly down to hide themselves, as little Ruth and her companion came towards it.'"

"*Martin Chuzzlewit*," groans Nobby, gurning.

"Indeed," Crispin coughs. "Let us depart this walled state of grace and grub for more stories." Melanie shakes her head and peers into *Frobisher's*, while the group files into Devereux Court and heads north.

"Ah, Fleet Street," rasps Crispin, "a dying metonym. Once this area defined the British press. The first daily English newspaper, *The Daily Courant*, was published here in 1702. All the newspapers have since left in search of less expensive places to park their scribes' posteriors and print their hairy tales.

"Here are the Royal Courts of Justice, built in Gothic style in the 1870s as a temple to justice. Serious civil trials are held here: defamation, personal injury. Eighty-eight courts inside, all open to you and me on the basis that justice must be seen to be done.

"And to our left, St Clement Danes. Hounded by traffic. Built in the ninth century for Danish men living in London. Rebuilt in 1662 by Wren. It's the central church of the Royal Air Force. The stunning nave and aisles feature the crests of hundreds of RAF squadrons and rolls of honour.

"Now," says Crispin, turning about so fast he produces a sharp squeak from his feet, "behold Apostrophe, a working re-enactment of an authentic boulangerie patisserie. Note the passage from Flaubert's *Madame Bovary* reproduced across this glass, with a crisp reflection of the courts behind the text and then the muted drama of customers conversing, reading, thinking."

"You mean this café window?" asks Dieter.

"Yes, this palimpsestuous screen presents a perfect merging of fiction and reality, of art and law, of history and fable. A tribute to stories as the warp and woof of Temple. A felicitous framing don't you think, Master Drew, my dearest hobbledehoy?"

"Whatever," says Drew.

"Schnell. Vamos. Time has gathered her britches and is chasing us down the Strand," says Crispin, and he leads the group back towards Temple Tube. By the steps to the station volunteers are handing out hot food to homeless men and women. Sprites of steam rise from each polystyrene container.

Dieter moves alongside Crispin and says, "You know, I'm not actually German. I'm not really called Dieter either, it's just a nickname from school. My grandfather was from Frankfurt, but I was christened Dave and grew up in Swindon. Melanie prefers Dieter because when we met she'd already been out with three Daves."

Crispin pats Dieter on the small of his back, draws on his hood and declares, "Circumvenio. I hope you enjoyed your perambulation along the cunning passages and contrived corridors of Temple. Come back and continue the story for yourself. Merci."

Nobby hollers "Confabulous!" and yomps off towards Charing Cross.

"Much appreciated," chorus Mikey and Peggy, and they walk to the Strand, bickering about baguettes. Drew, smiling beatifically, sticks his middle finger up in Crispin's direction and shouts "Outtahere!"

"Adieu. Auf wiedersehen. Gesundheit. Farewell," says Crispin, quietly.

Melanie is some distance away, dancing with a wind-tormented street map bigger than she is. Dieter looks into the eyes blinking in the dark recesses of the monk's hood.

"Crispin," he says slowly, "you are an untrustworthy guide. A fabricator. A knave. I've enjoyed every minute. But be careful what you invent – you never know what you might start."

"Thank you, Dave of Swindon," whispers Crispin. "And just you remember, always question what you're told by a medieval monk wearing sneakers."

EMBANKMENT

The sanctuary of shadows

Rob Williams

Why d'yew ask what time I'm up? I'm up at 7.30 mate what d'yew think, I've nuthin to get up for? I've as much as the next man to be up for and anyway, the gardeners want yew out by 7.30 as a rool, before the punters start comin throo, like. Yew don't take the piss. Yew keep yourself reasonable yew stay polite and by and large, they let yew be. Not like them what piled out of Heaven in the early hours of this morning; wailin like tortured foxes they was like dogs of war. It's the drink, like. But not just the drink. And if it weren't for these fences, if Martin and me'd been huddled up by the toob station instead of behind these discouraging spikes, yew'd be at the mercy of them dogs and their bottles and their foory. I've seen it, mate. Way they show their teeth. Kiddies of course you half expect that but it's not just them; it's men in suits and women in their finery. Seem to bring out the worst in em we do. Us and the drink, like.

It's a violent world. Yew only have to read the *Metro* of a mornin. I like to read. After the ablutions, like. See that squat brick buildin over there near the station? That's a rare public toilet what won't ask for twenty pence that usually yew ain't got. First thing of a mornin it's as busy as the station; full of fellas havin a wash and brush up. Yew think this is dirt? Well it is dirt mate obviously but most of it's tobacco stains or ground-in filth that at the age of forty-nine with only a sink in a public garden to rely on, we both might have to live with, you know? There's worse things anyway. Much worse. Yew only have to read the *Metro* of a mornin. But I'd still rather be in London than back in Weston, even just from a general aggression point of voo.

That surprises yew. It is surprisin. Probly the last time these hands were proply clean: Weston-super-Mare. Or the flat in Swindon, before the rehab and Bristol and that. That's when I started the beard, like. Sum of the fellas'll have a shave of a mornin but I'm as attached to me beard now as it is to me like, grey bits an all – it's me clock see, me calendar even and along with the days and the nights and the seasons, it's the only one I have use for really. Sum of the fellas they'll sit in there all day, crack a tin in a cubicle and drink the day away, but not me; yew don't take the piss. I'll nip in the station. Big shabby piece on the chessboard tiles; a pawn I am, rarely more than that. Pick up me *Metro* before the punters start comin throo. Does the flower girl need help settin up today? Not today she never but last Toosday or Friday she did and it was worth a blue spot and that's worth more than a fiver if yew know how to spend it. To be asked to help with the flowers or to hand out this or that outside the station, it's a buzz that is. Above and beyond the money, like. Yew can be useful. Yew . . .

Treat people right and they treat yew right, you know? What else yew gonna do anyway?

Just sit on the wall near the bandstand there and read the *Metro*. I like to read. *Down and Out in Paris and London* – you read that? I have. George Orwell, mate. There's a chap in that lives on Embankment. I like to read. Every day I sit there and I read about all sorts of things, terrible things sumtimes right here in the middle of London and I'll try to make sense of it alongside this: the toolips and the green spaces and even the way the traffic noise off Victoria Embankment gets suffocated by just a foo trees . . . Makes yew wonder about Noos, you know?

Makes yew wonder. Makes yew think it's miraculous, this place. Home. I'll call it that sumtimes, to meself like. "Home." It'll sound a bit stoopid even to an audience of that size but if this ain't home, then where is? Nah, Weston's just where I'm from, mate. And it's never give me this sense of calm, this feelin of secoority that yew gets round here. Well we all need that mate, whoever yew are. But that it can be found here, with the trains rattlin overhead just a short walk from the Strand and the screamin heart of Central London, well that comes as a surprise to me too. It can though. Maybe *because* we're in the shade of Charing Cross, you know?

Because we've been chood up by the mouth of that mainline fucking monster up there; chood up and spood out and forgotten about. We man a forgotten outpost here, those of us who live and work in this place and we treasure our secret we do, teeterin on the edge of the water like condemned pirates, last stop before yew drop down into the Thames. Didn't even exist hundred and fifty years ago. This yew'd know if yew'd read and re-read the information boards all over these gardens. I like to read. We was created only about 1860 or sumthin like that when they pushed back the Thames; from Cleopatra's Needle almost to the back of the Savoy, they *pushed back* the water like it was a wild animal. Pushed it back and created a sanctuary. For all them who need it, like.

Sum more than others mate yeah that's troo, troo enuff. This area it's famous or is it infamous for the homeless which is why you're interested I spose obviously. Used to be hundred or so bodies under Hungerford Bridge there, where them smart shops are now, before my time like ten maybe fifteen years ago. I'd still be in me flat then but drinkin too much, not really copin like. Anyway there was a city under there in them days. Embankment Place. But it's still a tourist area at the end of the day. The river, Westminster and that, Trafalgar Square. Yew see em all the while, sightseers with their expanding maps and bulging backpacks and gazes that try not to see certain sights, try to make yew a part of the wall or some sort of statue. But even they couldn't fail to notice an entire city.

So the cardboard got bloo away. Winds of change, exactly. But where did they all go though? Wherever the wind bloo em, I spose. But we're still here. In the gardens, mostly. Some'll go off in the daytime and come back at night but apart from a coffee and a bit of breakfast up at St Martin's, I'll pretty much stop round here. Day'll take care of itself mostly. I'll walk round, go throo the bins for sumthin to read or sumthin to eat and I'll maybe go for a drink if I'm lucky enough to have the money, over to the South Bank or the Charlie Chaplin at Elephant and Castle; but I'll always wanna get home or near home at some point before dark . . . so long as I know what I'm doin, like.

Mostly though I'll just sit. And think. And watch. I don't beg people, no. Yes I do beg people, but not round here. Not on me own doorstep. Sumtimes yew'll have to get out and about if yew've not eaten for a day or two, but mostly sumthin'll turn up. Yew might get asked for directions and that's a buzz too: bein able to help people out. *Here yew go, mate – take this.* You know? I never ask. I . . .

Every day I watch four five hundred punters come and go throo here, to and from their jobs like and good jobs most of em yew'd imagine, what with the DTI and Whitehall up there and Pricewaterhouse Wossername just here, the Strand beyond it. Do I envy em well I have done, I have done and to say otherwise would be a lie. But the thing is, the thing you have to ask yourself is . . . Are they happy? And I'll tell yew mate, take it from one who's made a study of these faces – they're *not*. They fucking can't be. It's rare to see smiles.

So what's it all about then? That's what I wonder. If they ain't happy, what do they do it for? So they don't end up like me fair enuff that's troo, but . . . What do they think of me as they pass by? Do any of em envy me my life? Do any of em even see me, is more the question. Most won't even swap a Good Mornin with yew, just in case it costs em. Rather stare at their own feet than risk noticin these bootiful gardens or this ungainly man with the unruly beard. And it don't; it don't cost nuthin. Makes yew wonder. Could I change? Do I want to change?

You know?

I don't know.

I just roll a smoke and I watch em go by. Watch it all go by. Most people leave yew alone cos they wanna be left alone theirselves. Yew find that generally in life, whether you're in prison or in Embankment Gardens.

Yew can smell a bit sumtimes, fair enuff . . .

Sumtimes you can look at the shape of your day and at what you've actually don with it, at what you've don with your life like, and it can scare yew. Make yew panic about all sorts of things that ordinarily are kept at bay by hunger and more usually thirst, same way the noise of a hectic city is kept at bay by these trees and them gates. It's all so fragile. But it soon passes. About as quick as the punters headin back to the station after work . . . What have they don with their day? It's all the same innit, looked at from a certain height. We all of us need secoority, mate. As keenly as we need to eat, like.

Course you do, course you get hungry! Specially round here. Lookin up Villiers Street of a lunchtime, it's like watchin piglets round a sow's teat it's a movin carpet of empty bellies and every shop is a café or a sandwich bar. They're good to yew in the evenings though sum of em, sumtimes way before they close even. Sum more than others obviously but most don't like waste. People are basically good in my opinion. Yew watch em long enough and yew almost can't help but come to that conclusion, even if you don't want to. What I mean is I have a high level of distrust and that's there for a reason like but it's also largely unfounded, you know? A practical necessity that's debunked on an almost daily basis. There's sumthin good about that.

People.

Night-time they all swarm back but not to feed now. Some'll go to the bars and pubs and later the clubs but mostly they're on the way back to the station. They wanna get home now and that's where you're fortunate, one of the ways: you're already there. I don't envy them their shelters by and large no I don't and that's nuthin to do with money or even responsibility. It's to do with the fact that this home of mine it's alive – and so it never gathers dust. My decor shifts throughout the day as layers are added and others are stripped away, constantly changin the landscape like the seasons alter the gardens and the wood on this bench. Winter. That's my season. Gets dark earlier so its easier to get your head down. And there's less people about cos of the cold, so it's safer. Rain is welcome for the same reason. If yew've a good sleeping bag and groundsheet – and if you're not just a fly-be-night then there's no reason why yew shouldn't have – then the cold holds no fears for yew. What does? Them packs of drunken dogs wantin to give you hard time just for bein, that's what. But yew go and find Martin. Each layer of this commoonity it's a commoonity in itself and at night yew seek out your own. Yew sleep in pairs. Secoority. Yew find Martin and yew sleep in pairs and yew put that fence between yew and the rest of the world. Think of em as curtains, mate.

I'll try to get to bed before nine if I can. Soon as the gates close like, sumtimes before. These new benches they've started puttin in, with the dividers built in to form seats – whose bright idea was that then? Whoever it was they've never been homeless I tell yew and they obviously never expect to be either. And they might well be right. But that's why the gardeners'll tolerate us, I reckon – I mean so long as we don't aboos the situation or wreck nuthin like the fly-be-nights will: because they know they're only a month's money away from a night on a disappearin breed of bench. Others might be further away but none are as far away as they'd like.

Is that why they chuck bottles? I dunno, mate. But in the darkness, once the whole area's cleared and the shadows take over, often my eyes'll fasten on the stars and me mind'll fix on the eternal, on that which endures. And sumtimes, layin here amongst all these monuments of great statesmen and soldiers and scientists and artists, I'll come to think that far from representin the dregs of Embankment, I am in fact its heart. Why me? Because I was here when nuthin else was mate, and I will be here when Pricewaterhouse Wotsit and the Japanese deli and Heaven have all been reclaimed by the Thames and washed away forever.

Not *me* as such, no – but souls like me. Peel away the layers particular to period and to culture and to the prevailin idea of what society should aspire to, rub away the modish like water on stone and what disappears is the tourist and the accountant and the media studies stoodent. And what remains is me. The man with nuthin but his beard. The man with no one but himself. Today you find me in the shadows. Tomorrow, who knows . . . This home of mine, it has much to tell about evolution. But it can't tell yew everythin. Not yet. No one can.

But anyway.

See yew in the mornin, mate.

WESTMINSTER

Liberty City

Tim Coates

The Times, 26 July 1833
Announcement
"Notice is hereby given that the public may view the new Tunnel under the Thames on any day except Sunday from 9 in the morning until 8 in the evening upon the payment of 1 shilling for each person. The Archway is lighted with oil-gas reflected by a large mirror at the externity of the finished portion of it and thus receives great light and gives the effect of completion to it. The work is dry and warm and the staircase to it easy and safe.

A pamphlet entitled 'An exposition of facts and circumstances relating to the Tunnel' which was presented to His Majesty by Mr Brunel at an audience last May, may be had at the office upon application for the same."

The tunnel had experienced two dramatic floods. It was the first attempt anywhere in the world to tunnel underneath a river. Such work requires a comprehensive analysis of the geology of the layers of ground, both at low tide, in the case of a tidal river, and when the level is at its highest. On one occasion, the river broke through into the descending chamber and Brunel's son only narrowly escaped; three others died.

The final plan was for a carriageway inclining on both sides of the river so that the complete construction was intended to be three-quarters of a mile long. Such a project required patience, skill, perseverance and money. When opened for public viewing, the work had already been under way for eight years.

Advertisement
"Lost, on Tuesday last, out of a gentleman's carriage: a French Black Lace Veil. Whoever will take the same to Messrs Swan and Edgar, 10 Piccadilly, or to Mrs Edgar, West Hill, Wandsworth, shall be rewarded for their trouble."

Parliamentary report
"In the House of Commons Mr O'Connell demanded that the proprietors of *The Times* and the *Morning Chronicle* be brought to the House to answer for a breach of privilege for publishing the debates of the House. He said he was determined not to submit to the despotism of newspapers. The honourable member then proceeded in a strain of violent abuse, sometimes of individuals by name, quite unfit for publication."

The debate that followed revealed that Mr O'Connell was not suggesting that reporting be banned; rather, he was claiming that what he had said on a previous occasion was not fairly reported by these newspapers. Unfortunately for him, the other members of the House who were present and had heard what Mr O'Connell actually did say took the opposite view and observed that it was better, in their minds, for Mr O'Connell to regret what he had said, than for the reporters to apologise for what they had written.

"Astley's Royal Amphitheatre

This Evening will be presented 'The Siege of Troy' or 'The Giant Horse.' Likewise a lively military and equestrian anecdote, in which the celebrated Herr Cline will appear, called 'Frederick the Great,' or 'The Artist and the Royal Rope Dancer.' Scenes in the circle: The Equestrian Chinese Juggler who will, at full speed, perform some equilibriums and other exercises peculiar to himself. Mr Ducrow's grand pageant and allegorical cavalcade of the Four Quarters of the Globe: Europe, Asia, Africa and America performed by 11 highly trained steeds, male and female warriors, richly attired etc. To conclude with 'The Caravan or 'The Driver with his Dog.'"

The Magistrate's Court

"A very curious incident occurred in the magistrate's private room. Broomhead, one of the overseers of the parish of St George, introduced to Mr Conan a young female, very smartly attired, who had endeavoured to add to the population of the parish, with a request that he would question her as to the author of the unwelcome visitor. The young lady who, in addition to a well formed figure had a profusion of very light hair arranged with great taste about a countenance, the *tout ensemble* of which presented a very attractive picture, pointed to a fashionably dressed gentleman and declared that to him alone were to be awarded the honours of paternity. The young lady, whose name is Miss Price, having made this avowal, sank down on a seat and employed a pair of very expressive eyes alternately in dropping tears and darting complacent glances towards a mirror which reflected at full length her very pleasing exterior

The uncle of Miss Price, who was present, begged Mr Conan to enquire of the defendant his real name as he believed the name on the warrant to be fictitious. Miss Price admitted that she did not know who the defendant was. Under the euphonious appellation of Charles Albert Hamilton he had moved and won her virginal affection, and though for four years their correspondence had subsisted, she had never been enabled to penetrate the mystery in which he enveloped his name and occupation. She implored the magistrate to relieve her anxiety by extracting the necessary information from her mysterious deceiver. The parish officer said he knew nothing whatever of the defendant, having only captured him through a stratagem planned by the uncle of the young lady who watched her to her last amorous appointment, and when the 'gay Lothario' made his appearance and appeared to fly into the arms of love, he made the disagreeable discovery that he was in the arms of the parish beadle."

"Mr Conan – Is your real name Charles Hamilton?

The Defendant *(hesitantly)* – Yes, that is the name which I have hitherto gone by.

Mr Conan – What are you, sir?

The Defendant – A professor.

Mr Conan – Of what?

The Defendant – A professor of motion.

Mr Conan – You give lectures, I suppose, on the laws of motion?

The Defendant – Not exactly, I mean motion relative to the body.

Mr Conan – Pray explain yourself a little clearer, sir. Do you mean you are a dancing master?

The Defendant – Yes, I do.

Miss Price – A dancing master! Oh Charles, pray ease my doubts. Who are you?

The Defendant – I cannot, dare not state my real name. That must remain for ever a secret.

Mr Conan – Well, sir, you must state your circumstances, so that I may know at what sum to put the weekly allowance.

The Defendant – I am worth nothing. I have been a merchant in odds and ends; I am a bankrupt, a ruined man. All I can afford is a half a crown, weekly.

Mr Conan – Are you married?

The Defendant *(clasping his hands)* – Married? Must I confess? I will speak the truth. Yes I am.

'Oh you villain,' said Miss Price, giving a theatrical scream and walking backwards and forwards before the looking glass. 'You told me you were single."'

The young lady was questioned as to the origin of her intimacy with the defendant and she admitted that it had been accidental and that the defendant, from the first, had solicited her to comply with his wishes, mentioning marriage only in case a certain event should occur.

"Mr Conan, having consulted with the Beadle, acquainted the defendant that he could not think of making an order when a false name had been given. He considered that it was due to the Parish that the defendant's real name and residence be known.

The Defendant – Oh heavens. I'll do anything rather than disclose my secret. I'll make any promise. I'll allow three shillings a week if you'll excuse me." (The reader not familiar with old English currency needs to be told that three shillings is not a great amount more than the previous offer of half a crown. It is only sixpence a week more: less than 3p. In modern money the defendant was offering the equivalent of £25 or £30 per week.)

Mr Conan did not appear to think that the last offer was in any way an inducement.

"The Defendant – Well then, let me implore you to have the room cleared, or to indulge me with a private communication.

Mr Conan did not think it was necessary to agree to either of the requests.

'Then my mind is made up,' said the defendant. 'I will trust you with my secret. I am,' said he, leaning over the table towards the magistrate and whispering in the lowest key, 'Charles Davis.'"

(Having refrained up to this point from passing any comment upon the enthusiasm or restraint of both reporter and editor of the newspaper in which this matter is recorded, the author should perhaps take a moment to draw attention to their participatory roles. Mr Davis was anxious that his name should not be broadcast, and here it is printed in the columns of *The Times,* which has a wider circulation at this moment than all other newspapers in the country combined together.)

"Mr Conan – And what is your business?

The Defendant – I am theatrical. I was formerly director of the Queen's Theatre.

Mr Conan – And the name you now use is ?

The Defendant – Charles Taylor

Mr Conan – Of which institute of dancing and under what name there?

The Defendant *(reflectively)* – Great Marlborough Street Academy under the name *(he spoke now very quietly but within the hush of the magistrate's room it was possible to hear)* Charles Theleure.

Mr Conan set the weekly payment at three shillings."

Negro Slavery

Having been elected a member of the parliament at Westminster in his twenties, for forty-six years William Wilberforce, a rich and independently minded Yorkshire politician, campaigned to end Negro Slavery, as it was called. On 28 October 1787 he wrote in his diary, with some sense of purpose, "God almighty has set before me two great objects: the suppression of the slave trade and the reformation of manners." Shortly afterwards he began to take opium for his health. The opponents to the abolition were those who made substantial sums of money from the dealings, and his morality was less persuasive than their wealth. Moreover at the time of the French Revolution, which coincided with the commencement of his campaign, his enthusiasm was easily labelled as radical and destabilising and to be avoided. He was resolute, but made slow progress. In fact from the 1790s for thirty years he laid abolition bills before parliament almost every year, but never succeeded.

Advertisement

"Female emigration to Australia: The ship *Layton* of 512 tons, will leave direct from Gravesend for Sydney. This fine ship is fitted up under the direction of the Emigration Committee, sitting under the sanction of Government, expressly for the conveyance of unmarried females of good health and character, from fifteen to thirty years of age."

News

"We understand that Mr Stephenson, the celebrated engineer of the Liverpool and Manchester railway is now at Paris making arrangements for the construction of a railway between Calais and that capital. We shall soon see the Liverpool merchant, by means of railways, making his journey to Paris in 2 ½ hours."

Yesterday a gray-headed old man, extremely miserable in his appearance, was charged before the magistrate with having attempted to drown himself in the river. When questioned as to the cause that had induced him to adopt so rash a step, he said that he was driven to having to commit the act through distress, having no means of obtaining a livelihood. His wife and himself had slept the last six weeks on bare boards and for several days had been without food. About five months ago, his son, who was also a boot and shoe maker, had died in the same way, having pawned a pair of boots he had been entrusted to make and being unable to redeem his pledge and unwilling to face his employer to explain himself. The defendant now saw the sin and folly of his conduct and promised not to repeat it.

On being further questioned by the magistrate, he said that if he had but the command of a few shillings to purchase leather for a pair of boots, he had no doubt of being able to earn a living.

A gentleman who was present gave the defendant half a crown for his present necessities, and the magistrate directed him to attend again in two days, when he would see what could be done for him.

William Wilberforce

William Wilberforce was so rich that he did not have to work, and when he was elected to parliament, he did not have to seek office as a minister. He married and had six children and his biographer reports that he was a devoted and playful father who cultivated a warm family life. Over the years he gave all his money away: some to help his children but most to causes and individuals whom he felt needed support. When he died he was quite poor.

In order for the abolition of slavery bill to pass through parliament, the British government allocated twenty million pounds to be paid in compensation to the men who owned the slaves in the West Indies. That was the price they extracted over forty years of resistance.

The abolition bill was passed in Westminster on the day that all the stories retold here, from official notices to music-hall line-ups, appeared in the newspaper: 26 July 1833, which was a Friday. The debate itself was spoiled by Mr O'Connor, who took such great exception to the reporting of newspapers that he tried very hard to have them banned and fined. Over the course of the several days of the debate on the matter of slavery, against the advice of the experienced politicians, he insisted on pursuing these journalists with all the means open to a member of parliament. But his colleagues, in the end, firmly defeated him. Reporting of parliament at that time was entirely conducted by men with notebooks who included many famous writers among their number: Dickens and Thackeray to name two.

So 26 July is truly the day of liberty in Westminster, for as well as marking out a moment in the progress of freedom of the press, it brought triumph after nearly fifty years of struggle for one of the most honourable men that Britain has ever known. Not only did he show nobility in his mind, but he demonstrated persistence and resolve in his actions, and the world is better for them. Sadly, William Wilberforce died only three days after the final passage of the anti-slavery bill, but he knew about it and was pleased. His monument is in Westminster, in the Abbey.

The result of his work is to be seen all over the world, and not least at Westminster, which greets visitors from its every corner. It is Liberty City.

Surrey Zoological gardens

"Under the immediate patronage of Her Majesty the Queen, the second anniversary of the opening of these gardens will be celebrated this Monday and Tuesday by a grand fancy fair and rural fete. A full military band, Weippert's Quadrille band, and the Russian Horn Band are engaged on this occasion. On each day of the fete the celebrated Miss Clarke will make the wonderful ascent on the rope to the topmost trees on the island. The French Hercules will perform his surprising feats of strength and juggling with other novelties. Admission 1 shilling. July 26, 1833."

Isambard Kingdom Brunel's tunnel under the Thames carries the London Underground from Wapping to Rotherhithe and back.

Carving out a controversy

David May

Rising above St James's Park station is 55 Broadway, the headquarters of Transport for London. This is one of London's most symbolic buildings: an early-twentieth-century temple to the art of transport that remains virtually intact as the enduring legacy of a small group of remarkable men who believed in the power of public art to enrich lives.

At the centre of the story are three radical figures: Frank Pick, the Underground's chief administrator, often described as the most powerful patron of the avant garde of his time; Charles Holden, architect of 55 Broadway, St James's Park and many of our other well-known London Underground stations; and the modernist sculptor Jacob Epstein, whose work polarised opinion and provoked public uproar throughout his career.

By the mid 1920s, the Underground Group had grown into one of the world's biggest public enterprises, and its board decided that St James's Park should be the centre of its bus, local railway and underground operations across London. Its existing headquarters at St James's, Electric Railway House, would be replaced by an efficient modern office block housing the centralised management and complex secretariat of the London Transport empire. Clearly influenced by American skyscrapers, it was intended to be the tallest building in London, with light, open-plan offices. Construction lasted from 1927 to 1929.

Pick held strong views on the power of good design. His keen interest in the Arts and Crafts movement, and latterly the work of the Bauhaus Group, had resulted in what was one of the world's first integrated corporate identities for the London Underground. Everything from the typeface and logo to rolling stock, buildings and posters came under his direction. Holden was also steeped in Arts and Crafts values, but had embraced modernism and a design philosophy based on fitness for purpose.

Yet Holden found it difficult at first to work up any enthusiasm for the project. Fifty-five Broadway was an awkward site, a rough triangle of land above St James's Park station bounded by Broadway, Tothill and Palmer Street. As he later admitted, "It was shapeless and irregular and plan after plan was abandoned as being too dull."

The solution, when it came, was simple. Thinking about the need of office workers for a short cut across the site to the Tube station, Holden decided to take a risk and make a thoroughfare through the building. He decided to adopt a cruciform design: the shape of a cross. Suddenly, the building made sense: "I remember the thrill of those two crossed lines on the paper and all that they implied: order out of chaos, a building with few corridors, perfect light and air to the offices and a plan that could almost be said to design itself externally."

To comply with local building regulations, the upper storeys of 55 Broadway had to be stepped back above the seventh, ninth and tenth floors, so instead of sitting heavily on the ground, the building appears to soar heavenwards, a cathedral on the Circle Line. Just as skilled stonemasons decorated medieval churches as they worked on site, Holden wanted the façade of his revolutionary new building to be adorned with the finest examples of modern sculpture to balance its strong vertical lines.

Two themes were chosen for the sculptures. The Four Winds was to be a series of eight bas-relief carvings high on the seventh floor of the building's four wings. The much larger and more prominent Day and Night were to face east and west on the second floor above the main station entrance. "About the sculpture in general Pick gave me a free hand," wrote Holden in a 1953 letter, "and I arranged the commissions among a number of sculptors so as to represent the whole or nearly the whole field of contemporary sculpture." Six of the leading modern sculptors of the day – Eric Gill, Henry Moore, Alfred Gerrard, Samuel Rabinonvitch, Eric Aumonier and Allan Wyon– had been commissioned to create the Four Winds. All were chosen because they carved directly into stone. Once preliminary sketches had been approved, the sculptors were given a free hand to express their ideas. Eric Gill was to oversee the whole group as well as carve three pieces of his own. For Henry Moore, initially sceptical about taking on a commercial job, the commission was his first public work.

This left the issue of who would sculpt the prominent entrance sites: Day on the Broadway side facing the rising sun, and Night overlooking the Petty France entrance, facing the setting sun. Holden later wrote that Pick told him he could go to whoever he liked for the Winds, *"but no Epstein!"* Holden had always wanted to use the New York–born sculptor, viewing him as a raw Whitmanic genius who drew his inspiration from ancient civilisations in Egypt, Asia, Central America and especially Africa. But Pick had never shared his enthusiasm, saying years later that he was "thoroughly tired of Epstein's ugly women," though he always joined Holden in defending the sculptor's right to express his unique artistic vision.

After a little time, Pick enquired what Holden had done about Day and Night.

I replied that I would like him to look at some models.
"Where?" he asked apprehensively.
"At Epstein's," I replied.
"I said I would not have Epstein."
"You need not have Epstein. I only ask you to come and see the models."
Pick saw the models, deliberated, and phoned Holden to tell him to go ahead. "There was no argument, no persuasion, and Epstein was ultimately employed rather to my surprise for Night and Day."

In the event, Epstein proved a controversial choice. Holden, who had first commissioned him in 1908 for a frieze on the new headquarters of the British Medical Association in the Strand, admitted that working with him was an adventure. Epstein intended his sequence of 18 eight-foot-high statues to represent the ages of man, and the work featured men with exposed genitals, women with sagging breasts and a foetus. The sculptures provoked a storm of protest from conservative critics, led by the *Evening Standard*. This was the start of what Epstein was to describe as his thirty-year war with conservatism. But it was the sensual bas-relief of Rima, commissioned by the Royal Society for the Protection of Birds as a memorial to the nature writer W. H. Hudson that provoked the fiercest controversy when it was unveiled in Hyde Park in 1925. The *Daily Mail* branded it "The Hyde Park Atrocity" and it was smeared with green paint by a gang of protestors.

Pick and Holden had been among those who publicly defended Epstein's work. To employ such an uncompromising modern Jewish artist on such an important building as 55 Broadway, at a time when fascism and communism were in the ascendant across Europe and Asia, was sure to generate worldwide interest in the new building. Holden was aware that he and Pick would be accused of courting controversy, but maintained, "If I didn't believe in Epstein we should not wish to employ him. No! We *risked* publicity but we didn't seek it."

At the site, Holden created an air of mystery by smuggling Epstein in and introducing him as "the sculptor," saying that it would not do for him to be known before he started work because "Dark forces might upset things." So it was with some nervousness that George Eland, an accountant and auditor for the Underground Group, clambered over the scaffolding onto the second-storey parapet during the bitter winter of 1928 and approached a shed where Epstein was working on Day. "I screwed up my courage to have a look at him . . . He looked round with a glare and pointed his chisel to the door . . . still I did see him chipping away at the solid block. We were told that after working the whole day he would go home and collapse onto a couch."

Epstein was indeed exhausted and often ill because of his working conditions. He was also wary of intruders. Journalists had been trying to sneak a glance at the work, and reported that he could be seen "muffled and mysterious entering the locked hut on the new Underground building where he is working in extreme secrecy." His caution was warranted. When the scaffolding came down, Day provoked "storms of criticism, rising at times into terms of full-blooded abuse" according to the *Manchester Guardian*. The *Daily Telegraph* called it "meaningless"; the *Daily News* was "staggered." The architect Sir Reginald Bloomfield wrote, "Bestiality still lurks below the surface of our civilisation, but why parade it in the open, why not leave it to wallow in its own primeval slime?" More headlines followed when hooligans bombarded the piece with tar-filled bottles.

Epstein believed that his work should speak for itself, but he did explain his intentions for the group:

> *The idea of Night was to impart a vast, elemental, or primitive feeling to the group. The large figure of the woman symbolizes Night – not the night of night clubs but repose and rest. The recumbent male figure symbolises Man – man reposing. Day was . . . a figure of the father in nature where the man-child, facing the light, still holds on to the father and the whole is revealed by the movement of the sun as the forms are revealed. . . . Such a subject must inspire awe. The sculptor is bound by the form of the building. However much people may dislike Day and Night no one can deny that they form very definitely part of the mass of the building.*

Holden described the finished carving of Day as "great elemental stuff, ugly perhaps, deformed perhaps, unnecessarily so in some respects, but as alive and pulsating as Van Gogh's sunflower and shouting robust delight and adventure in every cut of the chisel."

But after the works were unveiled, demands for their removal grew louder. The Underground board held a tempestuous debate in July 1929. Angry shareholders had written in protest, and the board felt that Pick and Holden had deliberately dragged them into a scandal. It was proposed that the sculptures be taken down; one director offered to fund replacements. Pick offered his resignation, but was given a few days' grace to talk to Holden and see whether Day could be modified to meet the objections.

"The story went round," wrote George Eland thirty years later, "that Epstein, in his usual manner, endowed the child with genitals of such enormous dimensions that FP [Frank Pick] had it conveyed to him that if he chipped about a [word crossed out] cut off – it would be more seemly. That may not be true, but I remember FP telling me, when letters of denunciation were pouring in, that he admitted Epstein was 'provocative' and that in fifty years the whole might be removed – meanwhile we are talked about."

Christian Barman, a former editor of *Architectural Review*, was appointed by Frank Pick as head of publicity for London Transport. In his biography of Pick, he wrote, "At Pick's urgent request Holden agreed to speak to the sculptor. There is a passage in Epstein's autobiography which suggests Epstein did indeed chip one and a half inches from the boy's genitals."

Yet this conflicts with Barman's own investigations into the story. In the early 1950s he wrote to Holden to check out the whole episode. The correspondence survives in the Transport for London Library:

> *My dear Holden*, wrote Barman, *I wonder whether you could throw some light on some rather unreliable information I have about the Epstein Sculptures on 55 Broadway.*
>
> *I have recently been told that Epstein was disappointed to find how little public attention was attracted by "Night" and that he therefore set out deliberately to make "Day" more provocative of public comment. You may possibly remember whether any thing of this kind happened.*
>
> *I have however been assured that the anger of the Underground Directors was only calmed when Epstein was persuaded to perform a small operation on the anatomy of "Day" and that, in fact, he removed one and a half inches of the offending portion. I do not think I should repeat the story unless I can get some confirmation of it and I thought I would consult you before going to Epstein.*

Holden replied:

> *I can understand the Directors being upset by the press criticism – that was natural and inevitable but Pick did not enlarge upon it to me and there was no going back. I don't know anything about your third paragraph but I very much doubt its accuracy.*

So did Epstein make the cut? Pick and Holden's decades-long defence of Epstein's vision and integrity suggests not. Given that all three men believed fervently in artistic freedom, the whole controversy could be regarded as a calculated effort to cause a public outcry and ignite a debate about freedom of expression in relation to the kind of works that would soon, in Germany and the Soviet Union, be denounced as degenerate art. For Epstein, the consequences of the row lingered for a long time.

The University of London refused to let Holden use him on its new Senate building, and it was twenty years before he received another public commission.

There were close echoes of the Day scandal just four years later when Eric Gill's carving of Ariel and Prospero was unveiled over the entrance of Broadcasting House, the BBC's new headquarters in Portland Place. Ariel was so well endowed that the MP for St Pancras felt moved to declare the figures "objectionable to public morals and decency." Popular rumour had it that Lord Reith prevailed upon Gill to cut the boy down to size, though no conclusive proof exists in the BBC archives, and when Gill was interviewed some time later he insisted he had carried out the commission to the letter. Nevertheless, Gill's story, like Epstein's, has persisted down the years, a testament to the enduring power of radical public art to provoke debate long after the death of its creators.

The final words of this story should go to Holden:

I prefer to say it in stone or on bricks and mortar or in any other building material. I still feel that it is the only language worthwhile, for what I say now doesn't matter half so much as what the building itself has to say to you – and to the generations to come.

Notes
Frank Pick quotes are taken from correspondence and
Christian Barman, *The Man Who Built London Transport: Biography of Frank Pick* (David & Charles, 1955).

Sir Jacob Epstein quotes taken from:
Jacob Epstein, *An Autobiography* (Vista Books, 1955).
Jacob Epstein and Arnold L. Haskell, *Sculpture Speaks: A series of conversations on art* (Heinemann, 1931).
Stephen Gardiner, *Epstein: Artist against the establishment* (Michael Joseph, 1992).

Charles Holden quotes are taken from private correspondence, his contemporaneous notes and an exhibition catalogue.

VICTORIA

We are not
amused

Dan Radley

Dan Radley
Detention: Monday 20 June 1977

Before I start this essay, first can I say, with respect, that it's really, really unfair, sir.

I was not, as you said, "Deliberately defacing a coin of the realm," I was playing 10p Up the Wall in the playground with Christie, sir, which I admit might look like it's breaking school rule no. 6, NO GAMBLING etc., but only if we had been playing for money, except we weren't, we were just practising.

As I look around at my fellow captives in detention, many of them hardened delinquents, some barely evolved from fish, I can't help feeling hard done by. Anyway . . . on with the punishment. You told me to write about Victoria. (A much fairer topic, I admit, than the legendary 500 words on the inside of a ping-pong ball you set Harris.)

Victoria
If you want to know about the area around the school, where better to start than the school song?

> Our song the gift of DACRE names
> Which Anne, our Foundress, brings
> St Margaret's benefaction claims
> The aid of names of kings
> These first of sowers from whose seed
> The harvest now we bear: *Unitate fortior.*
>
> We celebrate James PALMER'S fame
> And bless his bounty still.
> With thanks we magnify the name
> Of pious Emery HILL.
> For what they built we build upon
> And as we build we sing: *Unitate fortior.*

Wander back with me, if you will, to Tudor times. sw1 is a no-go area. Devil's Acre. So when Lady Dacre endows the land to build a hospital and our school in 1595, everyone thinks she's crazy. Other benefactors follow. Palmer builds Palmer's Village, 1654. Hill puts up almshouses in Rochester Row, 1708. Then all the foundations come together as United Westminster Charities and the Improved Industrial Dwelling Corporation. ▶▶ to 1977 and here we are: the result of their devious social experiment.

Still reading, sir? I guess not. Bum, bollocks, boobs. I bet you read the first couple of paragraphs then gave up and went down the Phoenix. Being a complete fanatic, you might read the last page too, you bald bastard, so I'll wrap up with something historical, just in case.

My Victoria

A strange egg-and-chip pong hangs permanently over the terminus like a forgotten frying-pan. But there's still nothing better in the whole world than coming back with Ben after we've been to Selhurst Park and pulling into Victoria, *victorious*!!!

Sometimes Ben's identical twin Felix is with us – "I'm him and he's me" – and that normally draws us into conversations on the train with fans from Peterborough or Mansfield or whoever it is we've destroyed. It's different once we're on the concourse. Ben pulls up the lapels of his jacket to hide his Palace scarf in case Millwall are coming back from t'north or West Ham have been at the Bridge. If you hear the clump of cherry reds, you run. (Off the record, I think the silk scarf around the wrist is something of a bovver-boy fashion *faux pas*.)

I love the walk to Ben and Fee's flat, out the backside of the station into Eccleston Square, then up three flights through the Buddhist Society. Om. You can really feel the tolerance in that place.

Meanwhile, round the corner at the Bioscope in Wilton Road they're showing *Sweden's Language of Love*. Nice of them to put on a film for the tourists. There they are in the Angus Steak House, wearing plastic Union Jack bowler hats. Or on the top deck of an open sightseeing bus paying £2.50 for frostbite when they could see it all from the good old number 11 for 20p. But they don't mind because Victoria is a right royal variety performance. Hence our school being in Palace Street.

Unitate fortior

As fifth-formers, it's our job to walk prospective parents of next year's turds around the school. Last week, Stads goes all theatrical, gives it the big finish: "Ladies and gentlemen, please join me in honouring those pupils who gave their lives during the Great

War . . ." He turns the corner, swings open the doors into the vestibule where all the names are in gold leaf, and there's Barlow, smashing a boy's head against the oak panelling. *Magister pulsat puerum.*

When Barlow smiles it's as inauthentic as an Aztec bar. To his credit, though, he'd never have let the seventh Earl of Lucan escape. He'd have had everyone in the universe with even a trace of a moustache standing outside his study writing their alibis on scraps of paper. "How was it that at 9.45 on the night of 7 November 1974 you were seen bloodstained at 72a Elizabeth Street, a mere seven-minute walk from the crime scene in Lower Belgrave Street?"

Victorian values

Teachers get their knickers in a twist about bullying, but mainly it's just bundles.

And if anyone tells you they were in the Battle of Kingsgate Parade, they're lying. We're in biology last period and from the top-floor lab you can see all the Pimlico kids hanging around malnourished by the crates at the back of Sainsbury's and perched up on the Underground vent, just standing there staring up at us. So the word goes round, "Pimlico – fight!" But come quarter to four the entire school legs it out of the side exit and disappears into Buckingham Palace Road, quivering.

No, the only decent fight I've seen involved Cookie Monster. OK, he looks like a pushover. He's not. It's the Irish in him. Psycho starts picking on him. Throws him down the stairs. Cookie gets up and goes "Stag Place, now." Everyone's chanting "Fight! Fight!" Except no one's really counted on the Siberian wind between the office blocks or Cookie's terrible sinuses. Anyway, Psycho thumps Cookie. But Cookie's like Our 'Enery. So there's blood and tears streaming. But his fists are still going like windmills. Doesn't know he's beaten. None of the blood is coagulating, and at a certain point Psycho doesn't fancy it. He turns and walks off with Cookie still having to be pulled back. And against all the odds, you'd have to say, Cookie wins. Now *that's* a bloodbath – splash it all over.

When youth goes forth to run its race
Some gaze at learning's prize,

Some contemplate the athlete's grace,
Some go with half-closed eyes –
But happiest those who run with friends,
Strong clasped in friendship's hand: *Unitate fortior.*

Football lesson

The three of us – me, Ben and Felix – all used to sing at St Margaret's, the House of Commons chapel. We've sung for Heath, Wilson, Thorpe. And once the Queen Mum came and chatted to us at the Mothers' Union service. It was a bit like talking to Nana Paddy. She didn't make a compelling case for the retention of the monarchy.

Right there in Broad Sanctuary, under the shadow of the abbey where the ashes of kings are scattered, we developed our football prowess. Maintained by the clergy, it's a lovely passing surface. Fat vergers sometimes storm out of the abbey shaking their fists at us, but we don't take much notice. And if a *peloton* of foreign kids shuffles past, we challenge them to a match so we can show off to the cute continental girls by beating their menfolk. I still fall asleep dreaming of Veronique, the French girl who took a shine to me. "Interesting… *very* interesting!" Her pigeon English had that certain *je ne sais quoi.* I recall she had a husky voice, like Thomasina our cat choking on a furball.

Pass the parcel

My mum's friends wind her up by saying: "How can you let Daniel wander round London with all those bombs going off?" True, once you've heard that sickening rumble, the sound stays with you. But what's the closest we've actually come to being blown up? Probably 1973, Victoria station, bomb in a bin: three police officers injured.

Now someone's hoaxing the school. Judging by the timing, someone who hates physics. We all file into the playground. But how do they know the bomb isn't *in* the playground?

I keep reassuring mum by reminding her I'm a moving target, e.g. I'm generally in the station for less than a minute. Front carriage, second door for the exit; out through the "no entry"; first up the escalator; stairs three at a time into Wilton Road; check traffic-light phasing; hop from island to island; blur past the Palace Theatre. Carry on England!

If I am on an IRA hit-list, they'd better hire a sniper.

At the end of the year the school tries and makes it up to us with a seaside outing. This must seem a really good idea to teachers: "A change of scenery for the boys." Unfortunately, when the sadists try to show their human side they lose control. And once we've done all the interesting stuff in the first hour – played crazy golf, spent all our pocket money in the arcades, eaten cockles and fish and chips, drunk shandy, gone swimming, been sick – there's still another five or six hours of meandering around some dismal coastal town, longing for the train back to the bomb scares.

The Permissive Society

There's a sign outside the Alfred Marks Bureau in Victoria Street that says Temporary Secs Reqd. I doubt that. But the place is crawling in braless young women these days.

I noticed the phenomenon first on telly. There's Lesley Judd making a pencil pot out of old toothpaste lids, but the camera's far more interested in her bazookas. "Here's one I removed earlier." And what about Susan Penhaligon in *Bouquet of Barbed Wire*? I'm watching with my parents and my dad can hardly believe his eyes. Then, last Thursday, the hottest day of the year, me and Ben are walking down Victoria Street and there's a sound like the bloke from the BBC Radiophonic Workshop with a wobble board covered in tin foil pretending to be an asteroid shower. Suddenly, the heavens open. Thousands of women in soaked blouses are running squealing down Victoria Street, clutching themselves as if they're in straitjackets.

There's a kid in our year called Rasputin and I swear there's no one funnier to sit next to if you're in Slaggy Maggie's biology lesson studying the female reproductive organs. Or on an ILEA outing to *Cavalleria Rusticana*. We're all pretending to be cultured and he's drinking lager during the intervals. So when a female opera singer in a surgical boot goes and falls over on the sloping stage and can't get up again, he gets so hysterical we have to stick a hanky in his mouth.

There's something different about the way Rasputin talks, the music he listens to, his clothes, his hair. Says he's going out with a Chinese girl who "will do *anything*." I can't even imagine what "anything" might consist of. I mainly just mooch around not quite plucking up the courage to speak to Greycoat girls. Luckily, Rasputin's posse of ex-girlfriends appear to be under instruction to snog me because it's happened a few times now and I'm not entirely sure I've had anything to do with it.

Victoria station has been Snog Central for me up to this point. I don't think it has any romantic significance, apart from it's where you say goodbye, so it sort of forces the issue. It would be nice to think it's the cosmopolitan influence.

"Victoria. All change, please."

I heard one of the boys from the school rock band Axe is now touring with the Wombles. And some kids claim they actually saw Pink Floyd's flying pig break loose from the Battersea power station chimneys.

It's a sign: old music's dead. As William Shakespeare put it in *The Tempest*, Act II, Scene ii, line 140, "The isle is full of noises."

You see, girls want danger. They want Rasputin, not boys-next-door in Orinoco suits. My mum's trying to help by cutting my hair like I'm in a band and mending my school hockey shirt with safety pins.

She's also started driving a yellow Opel Manta S, the middle-class Capri. Carefully. Meanwhile, I think my dad's become a secret republican. He's having to redraw a "Taxman" cartoon in the *Austin Reed Home Magazine* because it's disrespectful to Her Majesty.

Last Saturday, mum tries Inecto Hint of Tint on her hair. I tell her she shouldn't go out. Ever. My brother says she looks like Dracula. But out they go with their friends – to *Emmanuelle*! Then end up dancing on the tables at Anemos.

Compare this excellent behaviour with our teachers.

They start off living in bedsits in Battersea. Then they buy semi-detached teacher housing in the suburbs and commute in and out of Victoria wearing the same tweed jacket until they die. Their lives revolve around it like bewildered moths round a flame.

There's Nobblyknees from Teddington; Dr Suspicious, former KGB agent, who lives in Lewes (we know this because Timebo Bumsquash got hold of his address and everyone in our class ordered him free Hoseasons brochures off the telly); then there's Half-an-acre living opposite his mum in Streatham – possibly the only fully grown adult in Britain with an entire room devoted to Subbuteo cricket. Bev is the exception that proves I'm right. He drives in by Bevmobile, a Ford Consul cunningly disguised as an ashtray.

Painted ponies

I like Victoria. But, let's face it, it's somewhere on the way to somewhere else. Look what stays. Organised religion. Royalty. The civil service. Teachers. Everyone else moves on.

When Auntie Pat (not a real auntie) stayed at our house, she sang us a Joni Mitchell song called "The Circle Game": "We're captive on the carousel of time."

But we're not. The three-day week proves it. Everyone was moaning but it was a right laugh.

I don't know where I'm going with all of this. But that's sort of the point. You can go on putting leather patches on your tweed jacket, or you can go and buy a new jacket.

Sir, when you set me this essay, you told me to grow up. On that basis, the detention's been a huge success: I'm now two hours older than when I walked in.

And so we've come full circle in our historical sightseeing tour of Victoria. And I didn't even have time to tell you about Browncoats (1738) or Bluecoats (1688) or why the girls (who were boys until 1874) are Greycoats or why we've been wearing black coats since 1728. And how the boys of Greencoats had to wear matching green mittens donated by "pious" Emery Hill.

(Mumbled)
The blinding years fall soft as snow,
The generations pass;
The friends who come are friends who go
Like shadows o'er the grass.
But faith grows strong if hope and love
With memory bind it fast –
(Big football-crowd ending)
YOOOO-NEEE-TAAAR-TAAYYY
FOR-OR-OR-OR-TI-OR!!!!

Positive negative

Will Awdry

French Alps

In the shocking sunlight, he cannot focus for long. A landscape 60 percent pure white demands constant readjustment. His gaze trips, changing the view like a TV remote.

An eyeful of dirty concrete pebbles in the receding snow at his feet; a squint away to the cat-scratch striations in the rock face, 2,000 glacial feet above; a crash-zoom to the stumbling, slow-motion clientele around him. Seeking toeholds on the hotel terrace, their movements are at once clumsy and precise, reduced to half-speed in ski boots. Spacemen and -women in the season's most fashionable colours, they lumber decorously, a lost tribe of suntanned Neil Armstrongs.

Amongst the whirl of this Alpine excitement, his eyes flick again. There is a revelation in the snowmelt. It is a tiny picture, a vignette. He blinks. Something is triggered under the amber of his eyelids. He is transported 670 miles – and 120 feet below ground – in less than a second.

On the fringe of dirty grass between terrace and snow lies a discarded rectangular battery half the size of a playing card. The make is obscurely continental, the label design a jagged yellow pyramid on shiny black. Two perfect drops of water sit on its upturned surface, evaporating in the sun.

Liquid and electricity together. Water and power, one above the other.

He smiles and says out loud, "Sloane Square."

He pauses before adding, "The Underground."

Elephant & Castle

Jammed into the subterranean office, there should have been six characters in search of an idea. At this first meeting, there were four: two students, myself and the photographic expert. It was the latter's office, bulging with cameras and equipment, in which we were buried. (Over the next few weeks and meetings, two further students were to appear. A Frenchman and an Englishman, they both oozed skateboarder chic.) Above our heads, the busy life of the London College of Communication thundered on.

Our task was to conceive a poster that captured the essence of Sloane Square station.

For now, Ann gazed studiously at each of us with Finnish intelligence; Rebecca twisted her tightly knit hair with a trace of Gallic insouciance; and Graham – Mr Photography – broke the ice with a breezy download of extraordinary facts about the Tube, aerating the stuffy surroundings. He had photographed huge numbers of Underground stations in recent years and posted the results on a website – *http://www.londonstation.com/*. We were in luck.

While we talked, passing students made brisk demands for camera this and darkroom that through the hatch. Institutional procedure ran through these exchanges, and yet, in a few functional phrases about lending protocol, Graham conveyed a consistent thought as he handed a camera to each borrower: "Now you'll have some fun."

The atmosphere thawed. There remained a curious international air about us, a whiff of the exotic in an odd phrase or unexpected reference. Our boundaries were clearly not just British ones. As a cross-section, we were as random as the passengers in any Tube carriage.

We edged our way into the traffic of discussion, somewhere between a self-help group and a tutorial. It was time to dig the dirt about Sloane Square underground station and sift for ideas with which to paint its portrait.

Our observations were broad and diverse. We learned that Hans Sloane lived from 1660 to 1753. He bought the parish in which the station stands. A World War II bomb killed more than thirty people on the station platform. The Royal Court is next door to the Tube station. It has staged unsettling productions ever since John Osborne's famous play looked back angrily in

1956. In 2005, no one ventured much onto the central island of Sloane Square, with its few trees. Mayor Ken Livingstone had recently announced his intention to pedestrianise the area. On the last evening of the perennial Chelsea Flower Show, Macbeth comes to SW1 and SW3. Thousands leave clutching over-bred potted plants and trees, a Birnam Wood set to wither in gardens across the capital.

Above all, there was the legacy of Peter York, the man who coined the phrase Sloane Ranger, so defining the area and characterising the typical Sloane Square Tube passenger. With witty compression, York nailed the inhabitants of the neighbourhood as a tribe sporting flat blue shoes, piecrust collars, stripy business shirts and chinless accents. On publication, the *Sloane Ranger Handbook* slipped into a million Christmas stockings and as many green wellies. The idea stuck. Decades later, it has yet to erode.

As we talked, it was clear that our group wanted to undermine this stereotype. Little stands of opposition were carefully voiced. Rebecca conjured her grandmother into the room with a simple speech. This delicate elderly lady with an address just off the King's Road defied the stereotype absolutely. By the time Rebecca had finished, we had silently pledged to defend her honour against the brutal twenty-year-old moniker.

The inhabitants of Chelsea Barracks, it was pointed out, had also been anything but Sloane Rangers (the parade ground and billets were now apparently empty). Chelsea pensioners, thousands of tourists, millions of shoppers, ageing mods, rockers and past-their-best punks all failed to match the Peter York description. It wasn't true. It was all so *unfair*. We had to march into action to redress the injustice. In design terms, we had to man the barricades.

Before we were carried away on a conceptual wave of student protest, Graham led us firmly back to the Tube station. It was a pivotal address.

"You know there's a river that runs through it. Over it, actually," he told us.

Above the platforms of Sloane Square station, a 9'-diameter steel pipe traverses the rail lines. Inside this solid Victorian-looking conduit runs the River Westbourne, which flows from the north and through Hyde Park as the Serpentine. Unceremoniously rechristened the Ranleagh Sewer, the river has gurgled its way across the electrified tracks since the place was built. The station couldn't be constructed above the river, as the tracks would have had to be brought up to ground level at huge cost, blocking any building development. When that WWII bomb went off in the station, most of the deaths were caused by drowning.

Chairs squeaked as the group began to fidget. We'd found something on which to dwell over the coming weeks.

Milan

The British designer glanced from the projection screen to his audience to conclude his pitch.

Three men and one woman, they leaned forward politely. They seemed to do everything together, even dress. Their clothes were characterised by that finicky Italian take on the English country gentleman look: extra button holes, details and flounces offsetting sturdy tweed and corduroy. Ambassadors for the fashions they designed, their appearance gave him hope.

"I think," began the pony-tailed man with twinkly eyes, "your logo is very interesting. It is . . . inspired." He spread his arms above the conference-room table.

The Englishman threw back the remains of his espresso, congealing in the tiny plastic cup. He allowed himself to wait, in silent neutral, for the "but."

On the screen, the angular yellow pyramid jutted proudly over its shiny black powerpack background. Droplets of water ran over its surface. The legend "Sloane Square +–" sat proudly beneath, in an elegant, spindly face. It had been expensively rendered to look as though printed on fabric.

"You have captured an identity. The story is very involving, the Chelsea people, the ingenuity, the combinations of power and the water. I like the look, the yellow, the . . . the English quality." The speaker's voice dipped with the spoon he stirred into his coffee cup. There was a pin-drop micro-moment. "But it is, how you might say, not really *us*. It is not our dream. Our company is . . . we are not ready for such a *complex* idea. I'm so sorry."

"Bollocks," thought the designer, peering at the iced mountains through the window over the man's shoulder. "It's a gift of a design idea to a fashion label. Ungrateful bastards." His smile remained rigid.

It had been six years since he had first seen the battery in the snow. Somebody, somewhere, some day would buy it.

The passengers – those who weren't tourists – who stepped out of the train alongside me projected a fiercely proprietorial air. Seconds before, we had been Tube travellers, studiously pretending to occupy a completely empty carriage despite its crush. Now it was evening rush-hour, and this was their Tube stop. They walked briskly through the avocado gloom to the escalators, in a light that somehow fixed the ambience to around 1972 and duck *à l'orange* on Cheyne Row dinner tables.

Sloane Square may be only a simple, platforms-facing stop on the Circle and District Lines. Within, the most notable feature (apart from the prevailing colour) is the Westbourne River, tucked up in the massive iron pipe above one's head. There's the usual unremarkable array of posters and view of the sky. Leaving the ticket hall, however, I thought of those *"Departs, Grandes Lignes"* signs in Paris stations. The destinations presented to those leaving here are definitely impressive. For the fashionable, too, Sloane Street's designers parade every *Grande Ligne* going.

At street level, the view plays havoc with one's sense of scale: the vista is more village than city, but the magisterial quality grows. The theatre is next door, Eaton Square behind you, Chelsea's Hospital and Physic Garden within spitting distance; the red-brick gulch of Sloane Gardens is hard to your left. Immediately opposite is the mouth of that artery of British culture, the King's Road, and spreading its asexual petticoats about it, the pantomime dame of Peter Jones.

For generations, the King's Road has been more than a thoroughfare, a rite of passage. At school in the seventies in the green bit beyond the M25, coming into London was an Arabian Nights dream, the King's Road its forbidden harem. In the holidays, my coolest London friends got jobs at the Habitat café and sneaked us free bricks of flapjack. On a school trip to see the *Rocky Horror Picture Show*, a friend dashed by Tube to have an illicit trophy drink in the King's Road during the interval. Late back for the second half, he told us breathlessly that his pint had been proffered "With or without abuse?" When he'd requested "with," the barman had said, "That'll be 2p extra, fish-head." As for the shops, the unruly urchins are fast disappearing these days among the sleeker chainstore blow-ins.

Instead of inspiration, I'd found nostalgia. Seeking out a new experience, I went into Holy Trinity on Sloane Street just off the square. I was ambushed twice: first by the Arts and Crafts finery, and then, seconds later, by the precisely assertive sacristan. He talked of dark days of eleven-person congregations, near closure, applications to turn it into a club. Now it gleamed with well-attended love and wealth. You could have used the floor as an operating table. His clipped tutorial displayed a peculiar ability to voice the seigneurial line from a retainer's perspective. I left, clutching various leaflets, weakly promising to think about Easter services.

Johannesburg
Internal memorandum, Smithfield Distillers' Group, re Project Angelica

Please note that all work on this new product line, a lighter gin-style spirit consumer-tested under the brand name Sloane Square+–, has been discontinued following poor research results. The market will not sustain the launch of another positively-charged clear drink. Outstanding costs of technical development, name generation, design and marketing consultancy are to be moved into supernumerary costs outstanding for 2014.

Elephant & Castle
In the end, we stuck with the Westbourne. The river above the electrified tracks was too extraordinary to ignore. It provided the geographically precise accent to set the station apart from its 26 Circle Line cousins.

There had been other thoughts. A mirrored poster to capture the vanity of Sloane Square played to the York camp. A bagatelle game – a green baize-covered board with little enclosures of nails to capture a marble fired from a trigger in a French precursor of pinball – had also been suggested. Each nail trap was to have been one of the many local landmarks.

We had considered photomontages: identity parades to subvert the perceptions of the Sloanie cliché and intriguing 360° images. But we kept coming back to the Westbourne River in the Ranleagh Sewer.

In our final design, a column of clear water ran across a shiny live rail cushioned on a ceramic circuit-breaker, a visual echo of a lifebuoy.

As for our group, we'd enjoyed our Underground sessions in our underground room. As we said our goodbyes, I don't think any of us knew what we'd learned. The students had been looking to showcase work for their degree shows. Graham had been fascinated by the Tube from the start. As for me, a Tube commuter for 23 years, it had been one of the most enjoyable trips I'd ever made on the Underground.

Sloane Square Tube station is a portal to such myriad possibilities; we'd barely touched the surface. We couldn't hope to create an all-inclusive snapshot for every visitor. In the end, we had devised a graphic symbol of what makes our allotted station that little bit different. Leaving the college, I bumped into a vaguely familiar designer, a man I see now and then. I told him about our project and for a moment he seemed fascinated.

Then he was gone, muttering something about buying ski gear.

Valdivia, Chile

The government minister pressed the button, smiling broadly for the unblinking eyes of a dozen webcams before him. A few journalists and dignitaries clapped, along with an incongruous Australian tourist who had somehow made his way through the gate while trying to find the beach. Security had already snapped a discreet X-ray and notified all present that he wasn't a threat.

"When this company began operations eight years ago, we fully supported their efforts to generate electricity from the ocean," the minister said carefully. Oratory was not his strong suit. "It was a natural addition to our hydroelectric resources." He scratched himself absent-mindedly, staring out to sea as he tried to remember the briefing from his assistant.

"I am proud to open the company's third wave-power generating station. From today, around 16 percent of all electricity generated in Chile will come from the sea. This is in line with our international commitment made at the Penang 2030 conference."

He tugged at a string. A curtain opened to reveal a plaque displaying the power company's logo: a black battery overlaid with a bright yellow pyramid and beneath it, in elegant, manicured type, the name Sloane Square +−.

SOUTH KENSINGTON

The greenhouse effect

Martin Gorst

Welcome to one of the largest cultural centres in the world. Each year over eight million people flock to South Kensington to visit the Natural History Museum, the Science Museum and the V&A. Thousands more attend concerts at the Albert Hall, or study at Imperial College. But as you step out of South Kensington tube into the artistic and scientific quarter of London, spare a thought for the giant water lily and the nineteenth-century gardener who made it all possible.

It's June 1850. Henry Cole, an energetic forty-one-year-old civil servant with a passion for promoting British design, has a problem. Ten months earlier, at a meeting with Prince Albert, he boldly suggested that London should host an international exhibition. The Prince liked the idea, the Queen established a Royal Commission to manage the project, Albert was made president, and Cole was appointed to its executive committee. At first, things went well. Cole toured the country persuading wealthy businessmen to fund the enterprise. The commission invited all the countries of the world to send exhibits, and chose a site in Hyde Park.

But now Cole faces a crisis. With the opening day looming, he has no building to house the exhibition – and not even a plan for one. The competition to design a structure ended in farce. Architects, engineers and members of the public submitted 245 designs. The commission rejected them all, declaring that none met the stringent requirements. The exhibition hall had to be cheap and quick to build, it had to be fireproof, it had to fit around the existing trees in Hyde Park, and most important, it had to be easily dismantled once the exhibition was over.

With time running out, the committee had produced its own design: a long brick building with a large iron dome. Unfortunately, it came no nearer to meeting the committee's own requirements. It was hugely expensive, called for 15 million bricks that there wasn't time to manufacture, and would take months to dismantle. It was totally impractical, and Cole's dream of a glorious international exhibition was fading fast. But help was on its way – help that would not only rescue Cole, but ultimately provide the foundation for modern South Kensington.

It all began a few years earlier. On 1 January 1837, the German botanist Robert Schomburgk was rowing up the Berbice river in British Guyana when something floating on the water caught his eye. Paddling closer, he discovered a vegetable wonder: a giant water lily with leaves more than five feet wide. From the specimens he sent back to Europe, the English horticulturist John Lindley named the plant *Victoria regia* in honour of his queen. It was a spectacular plant, at least in the sketches explorers brought back from South America. But try as they might, European gardeners were unable to grow one to maturity. For a decade, English gardeners raced to be first to produce a bloom. Attempt after attempt ended in failure. For some, the seeds simply failed to germinate; for others, the plants began to grow, but died before reaching maturity. No one saw the majesty of the fully grown lily and its glorious flowers.

Then Joseph Paxton, head gardener to the Duke of Devonshire, entered the race. At six o'clock one morning in August 1849 he collected a young plant from Kew Gardens. By nine he was on a train heading back to Chatsworth House, the duke's Derbyshire estate. In a water tank inside a glass conservatory, he planted the precious lily.

Paxton stood more chance of success than most. For a start, he had the duke's vast resources at his disposal, but it was his engineering expertise that would give him the edge. He devised a heating system that would keep the water in the tank at the same temperature as the water in which the plants grew in the wild. It paid off: the lily's growth was prodigious. While specimens at Kew failed to grow, Paxton's skill put him ahead in the race to produce the first flower. By mid October, the leaves floating on the water were four and a half feet across. Ever the engineer, he tested their strength by having his eight-year-old daughter Annie put on one. The *Illustrated London News* carried a picture, and *Punch* published a poem:

> On unbent leaf in fairy guise
> Reflected in the water,
> Beloved, admired by hearts and eyes,
> Stands Annie, Paxton's daughter.

In early November, Paxton's *Victoria regia* finally bloomed. He had won. On 14 November he travelled to Windsor to present a flower and leaf to Queen Victoria.

Paxton's success with the lily was a triumph, but what happened next was extraordinary. The lily would provide him with the inspiration to design one of the greatest buildings of the nineteenth century: an economic wonder that would enable the creation of modern South Kensington. As well as being a talented gardener, Paxton was one of Britain's leading engineers. In the 1840s he had created the Emperor Fountain at Chatsworth, the tallest in Europe, but it was as a designer of glasshouses that he truly excelled. In the 1830s he had constructed the largest glass building in the world as a new greenhouse for the duke. Now his talents were called on again. The giant lily was rapidly outgrowing its tank, and a new conservatory was needed. It was while working on its design that Paxton came up with the innovation he was later to use on his masterpiece.

For the new lily house, Paxton drew inspiration from the plant itself. Until then, most buildings had sloping roofs; indeed, his own great greenhouse had curved walls that met at the top like arches. But the lily inspired Paxton to try something different. He reasoned that if the lily could support the large flat surface of its leaves, then he could build a greenhouse with a large flat roof. Strictly speaking, the roof of his design wasn't flat; it was made of long rows of glass in a regular zigzag pattern that resembled the stretched bellows of an accordion. This ridge and furrow structure gave the roof its strength.

From the outside, the new lily house was not particularly attractive: it looked like a rectangular box. But the innovative roof was extremely practical. It enabled Paxton to cover the 33'-wide water tank in a single span. The lily house was completed in the spring of 1850. At about the same time, Henry Cole and his commission invited the public to enter designs for an exhibition building.

The closing date came and went without Paxton entering a design. However, in June 1850, when all the other plans had been rejected, his opportunity arrived. He was visiting the Palace of Westminster with a friend, the MP John Ellis, when the conversation turned to the international exhibition. Paxton must have heard about the unsuitable design that had been cobbled together by the committee, for he remarked to Ellis that he "was afraid they would . . . commit a blunder in the building for the Great Exhibition." He added that he had a few ideas of his own. The two men then rushed off to ask the committee if they would accept another design. When they said they would, Paxton announced, "I will go home, and in nine days hence I will bring you my plans all complete."

His declaration was a bold one. The press and public were sceptical about the very idea of an international exhibition, and getting involved was like entering the eye of a storm. But Paxton had a radical plan. Not for him the heavy old materials of stone, bricks and mortar. His building would be a bigger version of his lily house: light and airy, with thin iron columns, walls of glass and a flat glass ridge-and-furrow roof. Best of all, it would be quick to build. All the parts could be prefabricated off site, transported to Hyde Park and then assembled. When the exhibition was over the building could be easily dismantled and the parts used again. Over the next few days Paxton fleshed out the design with the help of an engineer, William Barlow, who calculated the strength of the pillars and girders. At last, the drawings complete, Paxton boarded a train to London.

Winning over the committee can't have been an easy task, but Paxton was a skilled manipulator. While the commissioners were perusing his plans, he leaked them to the *Illustrated London News*. His design attracted widespread support, even winning over those who were sceptical about the whole exhibition. What swayed them was the practicality of the scheme, and the realisation that Paxton's easily transportable structure wouldn't become a permanent fixture in their beloved Hyde Park. To preserve the elm trees on the site, Paxton adapted his design to include a central arched hall tall enough to accommodate them. On 15 July 1850, the commission bowed to public opinion and approved his design.

The building progressed swiftly. A wooden hoarding was built around the site on the south side of the Serpentine. Fox and Henderson's iron works at Smethwick supplied 3,300 iron columns and 2,150 girders; the Chance Brothers in nearby Birmingham supplied 300,000 panes of glass. Workers started assembling the pieces in September. After the structure had reached its full height, a fleet of 76 specially designed wagons ran on rails along the roof carrying teams of glaziers. As the building neared completion, the hoardings were taken down and reused as flooring. Completed on time and on budget, Paxton's creation was a triumph. Queen Victoria thought it "incredibly gorgeous" and her subjects agreed. *Punch* dubbed it the Crystal Palace, and the name stuck.

On 1 May 1851, as the Queen opened The Great Exhibition of the Works of Industry of all Nations, a crowd of half a million flocked to Hyde Park. Over the coming months people came from all over the world to marvel at the building and the extraordinary treasures it housed: the Koh-i-Noor diamond, an astronomical telescope, the recently invented Colt revolver, waterproof garments from Macintosh, a model of Liverpool Docks complete with 1,600 fully rigged ships, hydraulic presses, and an alarm bed that woke you up by throwing you on the floor. Largely thanks to

Paxton's economical building, the exhibition was a roaring success. Before it closed in October, the Royal Family made more than 50 visits, and around 6 million people passed through the doors. With the money from admissions and the sale of the building – later re-erected in Sydenham, in south-east London – the commission made a profit of £186,000. It wasn't an astronomical sum, but it would be enough to transform the landscape of south-west London and lay the foundations for an entire nation's cultural centre.

As early as August, even before the exhibition closed, Prince Albert was making plans for the future. Like many of his contemporaries, he saw a need for better education in the arts and sciences. Britain was an industrial nation, and had got its wealth by innovation and design. For decades it had led the field, but now it was facing competition from overseas, particularly the United States. To stay ahead, it needed the best artists and engineers, and to produce them it needed the best schools in the world.

So instead of disbanding the Royal Commission, Albert arranged to keep it operating. At his suggestion, the commissioners used the profits from the exhibition to buy 87 acres of land in South Kensington. This area, stretching from the edge of Hyde Park in the north to Cromwell Road in the south, would become a cultural metropolis, or as one wag later called it, Albertopolis. Over the next decades, the area slowly filled with cultural institutions. More than anyone, it was Henry Cole who shaped its future as director of the first museum on the site, the South Kensington Museum. When the Great Exhibition closed, the commission inherited many of the exhibits, and the South Kensington Museum was built to house them.

From the start Cole wanted to attract a wide public, not just the learned and the wealthy. He installed gas lamps so that the museum could open in the evenings when people weren't working, and offered free admission three days a week. Visiting a museum, he declared, was "better for the working man than boozing in public houses or gin palaces." But he didn't seem to mind them boozing in the museum; to draw people in, he installed a refreshment room where alcohol was served.

The museum was more than a showcase for objects. The national schools of science and art were based here too, and Cole developed the museum for their benefit as much as the public's. The collection included plaster casts of Europe's most celebrated sculptures to inspire the industrial designers of the future to create beautiful objects.

Under Cole's influence, the area thrived and grew. A press campaign to move the National Gallery to the cleaner air of South Kensington came to nothing, and another international exhibition was held on the site in 1862. When it closed and the exhibition halls were demolished, the present Natural History Museum sprang up in their place. By 1866, the *Pall Mall Gazette* was reporting that "South Kensington is becoming the nucleus of everything scientific and artistic... London is spreading more rapidly in that than in any other direction." Two years later, the Metropolitan Railway company opened South Kensington station to cash in on the growing number of visitors and link Albertopolis to London's developing network of underground lines.

The Royal Commission continued to develop the area throughout the late nineteenth century. Most of the buildings we know today – the Albert Hall, the Science Museum and the V&A – date from this period. In 1896 the National Art Training School became the Royal College of Art, and in 1907 a group of educational establishments merged to form Imperial College.

Today, the area is said to contain the largest concentration of museums in Europe. Its original administrator, the Royal Commission for the Exhibition of 1851, still exists, and thanks to its shrewd financial management the original profit from the exhibition has swollen into a £30 million educational fund. Each year it distributes £1 million in research grants, and it has funded 12 Nobel Prize winners in its lifetime.

Joseph Paxton, the engineering gardener whose low-cost, innovative building ensured the exhibition's success, was knighted for his achievement. The Crystal Palace lasted another 80 years at its new home, giving its name to the area and a football team before burning down in 1936.

And the lily that started it all? If you change trains at South Kensington and take the District Line to Kew, you can see it growing in the Royal Botanic Gardens. They won't let you stand on the leaves, but if you're lucky, and you visit in late summer, you may just catch it in bloom.

GLOUCESTER ROAD

Random thoughts

On arriving at Gloucester Road Tube station 26 times

Gordon Kerr

The conscious mind may be compared to a fountain playing in the sun and falling back into the great subterranean pool of subconscious from which it arises.

Sigmund Freud

Shedding distance,
The blunt shape of our journey
Pushes a ball of West London air
Out of the tunnel towards Earl's Court
Where once, he briefly spent two weeks
Locked in a cell of his own construction
Searching for a lost key.

–O–

Exiting into the perfumed air
Puddles bruised with oil.
Light broken.

–O–

The light that falls on gable walls
Exposes more than the absence of form.
Within its beam
He would sit and dream
Of this space from which lives were torn

–O–

At the fag-end of the day
A presentiment of rain
Seeps between the mortar
As we shuffle into the station;
Men of tin and hollow women
With cheekbones like razor blades
And bodies like exclamation marks.

–O–

Like Gatsby, at East Egg,
Staring up the track,
The light shimmering
Like silk in the wind
Relentlessly red

–O–

Brakes hissing like a leaky hose
Eyes colliding and then separating
Worlds apart.
Delayed in a tunnel
The air growing solid

–O–

Gloucester Road haiku
Ruined by having only
Seventeen syllab…

–O–

Silent as a knife
A pigeon careens between the pillars and lands
Claws clicking on the concrete.
It then rises like a sigh
Dreaming of the sky, fallen crisps
And the sweet scent of chocolate

–O–

He knows this place
Like the veins in his hands
Or the tiny hairs
On the nape of his wife's neck.

There is a green-tiled corridor back there
One of the old ones,
No longer in use
Where he once saw something strange.
He told no one
And, to this day
He carries it around in his head
Like an unexpected parcel
Waiting to be unwrapped.

−O−

A tough day
He sits down heavily,
Creased trousers, scuffed shoes
Hair gel giving up the ghost.
He closes his eyes
And dreams
Of the skeletons of southern churches
Of the sound of a lone shutter
Creaking in the night.

−O−

Their clothes seem to be wearing them
As they stumble down the steps
Towards the Eastbound platform.
He clasps a Harrods bag
Filled with Special Brew
She has already bought
Her Travelcard to oblivion.
She holds her can daintily,
Little finger crooked
As if it was of the finest bone china.
Suddenly she stops
And eyes the dead emissaries
Lining up in front of her.

−O−

The day clings to us
Breath leaving our mouths reluctantly
And rising to the vaulted roof like incense.

A gentle hiss hangs in the air;
Mercury retreating into itself.
As the train arrives
We push politely forward
Desperate for each other's warmth.

-O-

Ghosts go before us
Through the turnstiles
Slapping their Oystercards down hard,
They are impatient to be getting on
There are quotas to be met
Deadlines to be stuck to.

-O-

The boys vibrate like tuning forks
As she traverses the platform
Accompanied by the whisper of nylon
And the yelp of stiletto on stone.
They shuffle from foot to foot
Trying not to stare
As she appears around a corner
Like a caught breath.

-O-

He stands at the barrier, like a treble clef
A ghostly presence
Somehow out of tune with his surroundings.
Thirty years he has been here.
One day it will end,
A brief coda without a chorus.

-O-

She has bought a bag
Which she has put inside another bag
(to be carried)
Which has all been put in her original bag.
But on the train from High Street Ken
She takes the bag
(to be carried)

Out of the bag
(her original one)
And pulls out the bag she has bought.
She puts the bag
(her original one)
Inside the bag
(to be carried)
And places both
In the bag she has bought.

–O–

Years could pass on nights like this
Spill like the pearls of a broken necklace
To the shadowed stones
Of the Westbound Piccadilly Line
They would fall
With the sound of cascading teeth
Or the parched rattle of shattered bones.
Or on nights like this
Lives could end
Down on the tracks
In the soft meld
Of metal to skin,
Linking the awful substance of death
With its medium
Its long-lost kin.

–O–

"Concerning the temporary nature
Of things," he says
Words squeezed between his teeth
Like toothpaste
Index finger scratching at the ether
The roar of the train a descant to his words
"We are less than nothing
In the scheme of things
We are only a tonsil
In heaven's throat."

–O–

There's a sound
Like something shifting, far away.
At the mouth of the tunnel
The air moves
With the silence of leaves in their season
Soon.
Soon.

–O–

Anonymous as ice
We stare at the curve of the glass
Of the tube train window
As if it means something.
Meanwhile, a Chinese girl bends forward
And ever so demurely
Picks her tiny nose
As the train sighs into Gloucester Road.

–O–

Once, swallowed by a different train,
She'd watched the sky melt
Over Ravensbrück and Auschwitz.
Now she walks these halls
When the night returns
Forever moving towards the ridiculous point
Of a Teddy Boy's flick-knife
On a cool spring night
In fifty-seven.

–O–

Something of the future
In the station today
Something like the universe moving
One inch to the right
Or a star bursting
Out past Alpha Centauri.

–O–

Outside
Cheap hotels lined the streets
Like bad teeth in the mouth
Of a stranger.

One day they lay in bed all afternoon
Breath becoming one,
The earth moving beneath them
On the District and Circle Line.

–O–

Head back
And absent-mindedly questioning
The precision of it all
He takes the steps two at a time
And leaps through the closing doors
Like a soul
Between the gates of heaven.

–O–

Late night,
Distant growls snub the silence.
A gentle breeze shifts a piece of paper
On the platform.
A train has just left South Kensington
Taking the air with it

–O–

Architrave, frieze and cornice
Glazed terracotta and square pilasters
Surmounted by an abacus.
An entablature
Gazed upon by bull's eye windows.
A cathedral, of sorts.

HIGH STREET KENSINGTON

Urban rides

Sarah McCartney

The space that the Underground station occupies once belonged to William Cobbett. Cobbett and I share the same birthday, 9th March, separated by 197 years. For these reasons I decided to write about High Street Kensington in a style based on his Rural Rides: *facts, some observations, a few rants and many digressions. I have no intention of establishing a newspaper, or of inspiring the workers to call for organised political reform rather than disorganised rioting, or of being imprisoned for sedition then elected to parliament, or of writing books and pamphlets while running plant nurseries and farms, but in researching the High Street Ken story I found it inspiring to discover a connection with someone who did.*

On setting out for High Street Kensington on a dismal February Sunday afternoon, I was disheartened to discover that the Circle Line was not indeed working that day; I had chosen a weekend when working men with loud voices and louder dayglo orange jackets were replacing the old tracks with new ones. I was thankful that they are being cared for, as I would rather pay my hard-earned pounds towards a good safe ride than niggle about a few pennies and wonder about my safety. I was a good deal less dismayed when I discovered that my journey would overlap with the Circle Line to convey me directly to my destination without the inconvenience of changing at Earl's Court. I am sure that a hearty majority of my fellow passengers were miffed to find that they could not complete their journeys in the manner in which they had planned them, but I *did not care!* I settled down to read my book but was immediately engaged in conversation by an elderly woman on my right who was disconcerted by the imposed change to her plans and asked for help in planning her journey.

As one who is somewhat of a Tube nerd, I relish the opportunity to advise anyone in need on their London Underground journey and I set to my task with enthusiasm. However, each time we settled on a solution for her – how to get to the Tate Modern, St Paul's Cathedral or Elizabeth Street where she may take tea with friends – the good lady would *change her mind* about which destination held the strongest appeal. I recommended that she travel to St Paul's, changing at High Street Ken as our train was to terminate there, taking another train one stop up the line to Notting Hill, and transferring to the Central Line eastbound to travel on their rather more modern, cosy trains complete with politely feminine recorded announcements. She would then be at liberty to descend to the river, cross the Thames by the elegant Millennium Bridge – which I shall think of for ever as the *Bouncing Bridge* owing to the unfortunate resonant frequency incident upon its inauguration – and take tea at the Tate Modern, where the view is superb and the cakes are delectable. (And the T-shirts of the serving staff match the painting on the back wall, which pleases me immensely.) On arrival at High Street Kensington (platform 4, what a rare treat!) I pointed her in the direction in which she should go, then she announced, "I think I shall be getting home now as they will be worrying about me!"

Too late, alas, as by then I was on the other side of the barrier, did I realise that she had *quite forgotten* why she had set out in the first place and was by this time heading for entirely the wrong train to return her to Ealing Broadway. Fortunately she was also heading for the office of the redoubtable Mac, a gentleman whose authoritative voice you may have heard over the public address system at High Street Kensington. Unfortunately, we mainly hear him announcing delays, but occasionally he tells us when the next train is due and cheers us up a little. That afternoon he was a busy fellow; his team were coping with hordes of bewildered travellers who had been hoping to emerge at Tower Hill with the minimum of bother, only to find that their train had turned left while they were chatting to their chums and ignoring their drivers. One severely bewildered old lady was heading his way when I saw her last.

My quest was to find a *garden*, but not the usual kind. One may walk west to see the ultimate embodiment of Queen Victoria's bad taste, the *Albert Memorial*, situated in Kensington Gardens. The unfortunate father of nine had requested that no monument be built in his memory, but the grieving royal widow flouted his dying wishes by demanding the construction of quite the flashiest structure in London. It is the more noticeable for standing in open gardens, not crowded by office buildings as so many of London's more subtle monuments are. "You can't miss it," as they say in popular parlance. Indeed you cannot.

Since its restoration and unveiling – following many years draped in a funereal and increasingly grubby pall of scaffolding and nets – the generously applied *gold leaf* could easily take an unsuspecting bus traveller by surprise and temporarily blind him as it catches the sun's midday light.

But that was not my *intention*. My search was for the magical and possibly mythical *Roof Gardens*, a place I had visited decades before, but had begun to imagine were not real, and existed only in my dreams. This was my second search; the first one was virtual. Naturally, I had consulted the *Google* before setting off. What did we do, ten years ago, to discover something? I cannot recall! Were we all more generally ignorant, specialists in our own small fields, consulting the books on our shelves or telephoning our friends for a snippet of knowledge we lacked? A mere ten years ago, fewer than one per cent of us in this land had ever *used the internet*. Consider this: fewer than one per cent of us own motorbikes but the others can observe from time to time what *riding a bike* is like and the advantages and disadvantages for ourselves. But the ignorant ninety-nine percent who had no experience of the *internet* were utterly bemused by it. How can one imagine experiencing something one has never observed? Badly, as I recall, with trepidation, with excitement and occasionally with *immovable reluctance*.

High Street Kensington station was once a garden; William Cobbett's experimental seed farm, where he grew the *Black Locust* tree before introducing it somewhat disastrously to the British countryside. He imported the *wrong strain* which grew ziggy-zaggy branches unsuitable for timber! He kept turkeys here for a while then moved them to the countryside as he was concerned for their health in the confinement of his large garden. If Cobbett observed the sardine-like conditions within a conventional turkey farm today he would raise a gang of supporters and march on *Parliament* (which would promptly debate the issue and decide to take no notice).

The Circle Line is shallow "cut and cover" rather than deep tunnel. Should you find yourself waiting between Euston Square and King's Cross for a signal to change and imagine you hear a peal of bells, do not be troubled. It is not the *ghosts* of lost travellers, nor the bells of hell from the depths of the earth; it is the parish church of St Pancras just overhead. When you travel close to the surface you will hear the more familiar and much more irritating sound of mobile phone texts being received: "You have three voice messages; please call 901 to retrieve them." Subterranea is one of the few places where we never hear the words, "Hello! I'm on the train!" Some of us go there for *the silence*. Let it always be thus.

High Street Kensington is open to the elements, a staircase descent below the level of Cobbett's *garden*; walk to the southern end of platforms 2,3 or 4, look east and a long way up, and you will see fully grown trees on top of the adjacent building, trees that are sheltered by the protection of the Royal Borough of Kensington and Chelsea, spilling out of the Grade II–listed Roof Garden itself. Mr Derry and Mr Tom bought the land on which you will find the current elevated garden in 1862, 27 years after Cobbett's death, and established their department store. How relieved he would be to find, perched atop an *Art Deco cathedral* to commerce, an experimental garden one hundred feet directly above his own. (Derry & Toms, though it had ceased to exist, was cited as Mrs Trepidacious's star sign in the 37th episode of *Monty Python's Flying Circus*: "April 29th to March 22nd. Even dates only." Is not Google a truly wonderful thing?)

Many who have visited the garden mistakenly believe that it is perched on top of Barker's – the next building along to the east – and so the myth grows. They have been there, of this they are certain, but on searching for it later they cannot discover the route! Did they *imagine* it? No, the gardens *were* built on top of Barker's but it was Barker's that moved *next door*.

When the gardens are not host to a wedding, a party or a similar exclusive occasion, then the common populus may visit. How pleasing it is to see that *Sir Richard Branson*, the current owner, shares his tranquil haven with his subjects. I hereby forgive him for wearing a wedding dress while attempting to match blue eye-shadow with red lipstick to launch his bridal company. Visit the Roof Gardens and you will forgive him too. I *defy* you not to.

1971: Biba, Barbara Hulanicki's retailing marvel announced a move over the road into all *seven floors* of the Derry and Toms building. Such was the ultimate department store, home to the fashion and rock aristocracy. It was fantasy made real, the assistants were so relaxed as to be almost supine and shoplifting was rife, perhaps contributing to its eventual collapse. By then, Biba's major shareholder was Dorothy Perkins. If one were to picture *Dorothy* as a woman, rather than a shop, then one cannot imagine her as a Biba customer! A blousy woman from middle England perhaps, or a gentle, waif-like creature, named Dorothy after her great aunt by Mr & Mrs Perkins who kept the greengrocer's shop in Chiswick.

Barbara and Dorothy were surely never meant to be friends.

In 1973 Big Business took over Big Biba. One pictures old school chaps strapping on the crampons, pulling out the ice-picks and scaling the sculptured walls to plant the union flag in the 18 inches of soil (plus drainage of bricks and clinker) that Ralph Hancock, landscape architect, put down 38 years earlier under the guidance of Trevor Bowen of Barker's.

In 1974 the Roof Gardens reopened; by late 1975 Biba was gone but, thank heavens, the gardens survived.

From Derry Street I walked into a plain reception area of six lifts and a security desk, plus potted plants placed protectively before unavailable lift doors. A typed paper notice announced that the Roof Gardens were open to the public; a friendly Irishman invited me to sign in.

"You look just like, what do you call her? That actress woman, wait a minute, it'll come to me. *Helen Mirren*," he said. "It's something about the mouth! Do they all say that?"

"You can be the first," said I. She is a good deal older than I.

Do not be impatient. The lift will arrive when it is ready and will transport you at its own leisurely pace. Turn left as you exit. To turn right would take you into the white pavilion where you may eat and drink at lunch and dinner time, but not in the mid-

dle of the afternoon. First, the *Spanish Garden*, reminiscent of Moorish Mediterranean constructions. Fountains play, but not in February. The knotted wisteria branches that twirled infinitesimally slowly took seventy years to wrap themselves around barleysugar brick columns. (I made a note to return to see them in flower.) The twin towers of the *Barker's* building look down their glass noses at the palms and eucalyptus but we look back and see that their flagpole has slipped to 30° from the vertical and we smile at their supposed superiority. There is a hum from the kitchens' air conditioning and the ceaseless but variable noise of traffic. We observe the spire of *St Mary Abbots*, the highest in London, built while Cobbett was farming the land over the road in 1820. Passing aircraft descend towards Heathrow.

Through two stone archways, past two supermarket trolleys parked incongruously by the kitchen's back door, into the *Elizabethan Garden*. High brick walls muffle the sound of a playboy revving his *Maserati* in the race from one pelican crossing to the next. A car alarm goes off. Everyone ignores them; let's make them illegal. In the carvings over the archways, cherubs sport suggestively with unidentifiable mythical beings. Bright pink cyclamen glow despite the gathering gloom. A blackbird explores.

To the south side I heard the rattle of a train pulling into High Street Kensington station next door. "Ladies and gentlemen, because of engineering works there is a special service operating this weekend. "The sound came clearly through a round window in the *English Woodland Garden* wall. The fluorescent flamingos disdainfully dismissed it, as they did all their visitors. Three pairs of exotic ducks were more curious; they splashed in the shallow water, unable to dive deeply enough to cover their feet and swim silently. One male hopped out to explore; his mate swam along beside him. How supportive they seemed of each other, staying in their bonded pairs. What can we learn from ducks? To take criticism as water off a duck's back, perhaps. A British couple, smoking and giggling, walked by; a quartet of tourists and I nodded to each other, uncertain as to whether we could speak each other's language; they almost certainly could and I almost certainly could not.

I descended when the lift deigned to turn up. Kensington High Street is one like many others, although potentially the *poshest* of the lot; its citizens are the wealthiest in Britain. It has a Boots and a Starbucks like Redcar or Ruislip. Stray along a side road and everything is different. Blue plaques are scattered generously along peaceful streets to show where the celebrated composed their words and music. *Ezra Pound* lived here. In a small, friendly café I took an espresso and Italian chocolate cake. St Mary Abbots' bells pealed with enthusiasm, tripping over each other to be heard. Two women, one English, one American, discussed school fund-raising, "If only we could get Dame Judy on board…" and the difficulties of spending weeks at a time away from their businessmen husbands. "It's hard to stay close…"

I thought of the ducks.

NOTTING HILL

Zoë

Lisa Desforges

It's too soon to be crying, so I bite down hard on my tongue while Zoë waits for her smile to reach full bloom. She squeezes her father's arm, breathes, and leads a train of red satin girls to where Peter is standing, eight years since they first met in Notting Hill.

Back then, I answered phones on Westbourne Grove, Zoë on Bayswater Road. We'd salvage what was left of the day at the Bonaparte or the Elbow Room, Zoë fluttering in, so alive with colour that the turning heads never noticed the details: the stubby, chewed-away nails that were my only clue she had worries of her own.

I'd ask, how was your day? She'd wave the question away, and then pluck from nowhere whatever conversation I needed to have.

The first day of our friendship defined our roles. My fiancé, abandoned an ocean away, reminded me of his existence by ending it. And as the other English girl in our California dorm, Zoë's was the door I chose to hammer upon, Zoë's the pillow-marked face that appeared around it, frowned, then fell at the news. She walked me to the cliffs where we watched the salty waves well up and spill over onto the shore. She waited until my tears ebbed away.

You should go home, she told me. What for? I asked.

That night she took me to a party, where we shared a bottle of imported vodka and snarled at home-grown sorority girls, belittling the carefree lives we imagined they led. Zoë indulged me and my guilt for a while, joining in as I pretended I had nothing to lose. Then slowly, green-fingeredly, she pulled my life back together. By the time we moved to London, I was ready to start again.

We wanted different things from the city. I was drawn to the exotic East End, its art and graft, its grimy newness, while Zoë settled west among the green parks and healthy prices of Richmond. Notting Hill was where our worlds overlapped, an Istanbul where we came to talk easily and endlessly, sharing our stories and plotting where our telephone jobs could take us. It welcomed us with the hospitality all its guests receive, and rewarded us with soulmates from its crowded table. Weeks after Zoë met Peter, I fell in love with Nick.

Just what you need, was her smiling verdict. Solid, and down to earth.

In pairs, we gained momentum. First dates became anniversaries, rent books turned into mortgages. Our jobs became careers. Zoë and I spoke more on the phone but less in the flesh, happy to fit our friendship around accelerating lives.

Until mine stalled again. After seven years, my down-to-earth life reached its depths. I was stifled and struggling, and Zoë was the first to know. Are you sure? she'd ask, over countless glasses of wine, reciting every heartfelt, flippant or drunken comment I'd ever made about Nick, the good and the bad, to test my decision. And when we were certain, she helped me find a cottage in convalescent Richmond, helped me half-fill the rooms with my share of the furniture, and the cupboards with crockery reduced to sets of three. She welcomed me into her and Peter's stable life, and set about piecing mine back together.

And now on a chilly stone pew, I'm battling with fearful, lonely tears, hoping they'll pass for a friend's shared joy. A few feet away, and not yet believing, Zoë and Peter blink at each other, her fledgling pink nails digging into the skin of his hand. Her voice cracks and recovers with words that prove how dedicated she is to him, how much stronger, more supportive, more enduring their love has been.

I bite my tongue and wonder why, in all this time, I've never known what Zoë's problems are. I look into Peter's speechless, smiling eyes and I realise she shares them with him.

The not entirely true story of a descendant of Horace Raynor

Laura Forman

Almost a century ago, two hundred thousand people decided to let me live. They might've thought they were putting pen to paper to save just one man. But decisions grow and grow. If you could unravel all the signatures from that petition, they'd form an inky lifeline pulling me straight from nothingness to somethingness.

Is that too much? Nah, don't think so. First rule of writing: lure them in with the opening. I've been tapping at my bloody laptop for a couple of hours now. It isn't my usual kind of commission. This is my own story, my personal slice through history. I've got to get it down so that girl, uh, editor, thinks "So that's how he sees the world."

OK. Where was I? Where am I? Bayswater. . .

I should've turned left out of the Tube station. Instead, I went right. Restaurant, newsagent, restaurant, newsagent. The entrance to an arcade that looked like a passage to the underworld. *Felt-tip pen and corrugated cardboard signs offering illegal refreshments to the already damned* – that's an idea. Carry on, carry on. *Hordes of girls wait to get into the ice rink. The generous sprinkling of glitter and the less-than-generous skirts make me think it's not just about skating.*

Right. The absolute right-wrong, wrong-right decision of crossing Bayswater Road. I'm in Kensington Gardens for a bit of a walk and a smoke and a think. I don't often have a cigarette but then you don't often find out you're related to a killer. So I'll let minor indiscretions slip. For now, at least.

The irony of coming here isn't lost on me. A couple of days ago, I was babysitting my sister's kids: half an eye on them, a quarter of an eye on my emails and the rest on the DVD I'd got for them. It was about the guy who wrote *Peter Pan*. He lived near here. Johnny Depp was playing him, prettily and platonically falling for the prettily dying woman played by Kate Winslet. I keep thinking I recognise a specific part of the park but it's hard to tell.

Yeah, so I was quarter-watching that while I checked my emails. A name I'd never seen in my inbox before was introducing itself. Telling me she was working on a new literary-cum-historical guidebook to London. Telling me she'd discovered some interesting things for the Bayswater chapter. Telling me she wanted to talk to writers like me who had some connection with it.

Not that I knew I had a connection with the place. East Dulwich is more my turf, it being the setting for *Overground*, my one collection of short stories. *Time Out* said it could've been written by "Ray Davies's fey younger cousin." Anyway, she seemed to know plenty about Bayswater and kept hinting about how I fitted in with its history. And it looked as if I was going to get some writing work out of it. I don't know if I would've been so keen if I'd known what she was going to tell me.

Finding out you're related to a killer shifts your worldview. But obviously I didn't know then that that was what this girl had in mind to tell me. She told me on the phone after we'd swapped a few emails. And here I am, complete with shifted worldview and a weird desire to get closer to some tangible history.

So it's out of the park and back over to the corner of Bayswater Road and Queensway. There's an old-fashioned clock on the street there, with an arrow pointing me in the direction of Whiteleys. All in good time, I think. *A short walk becomes round-the-world-in-80-restaurants.* It's all here. Pizza Huts cheek by jowl with Magic Woks.

I check my watch. Almost time to meet her. The café must be round here somewhere. Yes, this looks right. I slip into writer mode and make mental notes under local colour:

There are some sturdily, grubbily white ornamental chairs and tables outside. Think of them on a par with the well-washed foundation garments of a fairy who's had too many sugarplums and you'll be on the right lines. But a genuinely ornamental couple lounge around anyway and make everyone traipsing past look a bit lumpen.

There are a few seats with floral fabrics a little more grey and worn than they should be. The waiter's got the look of someone who knows how fast these two and three pounds we each spend add up. But bonhomie is off the menu.

I am a bit early but order anyway: black coffee and a plain croissant. There is a sudden slump into a seat at the table next to mine. A rumpled old bird. Flat brown shoes, stripy socks, a lot of beige. Some sort of meringue and cream mess. She is cack-handed with the spoon:

It conducts a limpy-lurchy waltz before it gets anywhere near the meringue. When it does, there's a fragile breaking sound that could be the hushed theme tune of osteoporosis. She pours too much sugar into her coffee because she can't turn the shaker back up quickly enough. The top of her coffee is a Richter scale for her hand tremor.

Embarrassed, she fumbles for a tissue to wipe her mouth, the table, the cup. I wonder if she can tell she'll be committed to paper in the next twenty-four hours.

The girl arrives at the same time as my coffee and croissant. The waiter hovers, a hunched reprimand of my decidedly unchivalrous decision to order straightaway. I scan her and she scans the menu before she's even taken a seat. Kind of studious looking, not disastrously so. Orange and frangipane cake and a lemon tea.

"It's always busy in here. You have to catch them when you can," she says before introducing herself.

And so it begins. She tells me about the guidebook and the Bayswater chapter in particular. She waxes lyrical about the inexplicable draw of middle-of-the-road cosmopolitanism and a few famous names who used to live here. Now she's onto contrasts: shabby flats with newspaper instead of net curtains opposite well-heeled mews streets. I steer the conversation back to what I'm interested in.

She'd given me the basic outline on the phone when we were arranging to meet up. I already know the who, what, where and when. Not so much of the why, but maybe no one will ever know that. What it boils down to is that a man I've never met, Horace Raynor, my great-grandfather, killed William Whiteley.

I can see them getting her tea ready, filling a sturdily English stainless-steel teapot from something like a samovar with French pretensions. *If that's not a cosmopolitan cameo, I don't know what is.* The waiter brings her order over, somehow managing to smile at her while sneering at me.

She's quiet for a second while she faffs about with the teapot, so I ask her about William Whiteley.

"Well, he wanted to be a vet or a jockey really, after growing up in all that Yorkshire countryside. But his parents got him a seven-year apprenticeship at a draper's in Wakefield and that was that. It was 1848 and he would've been about seventeen or so."

"So how'd he get from being a draper's apprentice up north to Mr Retail in the big smoke?"

"I don't think it'd be unfair to say the Great Exhibition was the catalyst. He came down to see it, his first trip to London, in 1851. I imagine he decided there and then he'd work up to having a shop as large as that. You couldn't buy stuff at the Exhibition, I don't think, but you can just imagine him looking at it all, wondering what it would be like to sell on that scale."

"Whiteleys sold everything, then?" I interrupt.

"Yeah. Actually, later on, when he'd been nicknamed the Universal Provider, he said they were equipped to 'execute any order that comes along.' So some joker ordered a pint of fleas. And got one! I reckon Whiteley would've collected those fleas himself if he'd had to. I mean, he built that place from nothing. I should tell you about that, you're making me tell this in the wrong order. . ."

"Sorry," I say, still smirking at the pint of fleas.

"He came down to London once he'd finished his apprenticeship. He took a couple of jobs and lived incredibly carefully, saving up enough money to open his own shop at 31 Westbourne Grove. He gradually spread out to the neighbouring shops. He married one of the shop girls. Everything was going well: six thousand employees and big profits."

"Sounds like there's going to be a 'but'. . ."

"Well, your Horace Raynor was waiting in the wings. But before that, in 1897, there was a massive fire and the shop was destroyed. The new Whiteleys didn't open until 1911 on the current site. But William Whiteley had been dead for four years by then."

"Come on then, how did my great-grandfather kill William Whiteley?" Now there's a question I'd never expected to ask. Somehow she's managed to polish off her cake even though she's been doing most of the talking. I give my croissant more of the attention it deserves, but if I'm honest, I'm more interested in the story.

"Raynor called in at Whiteley's offices on 24 January 1907. He said he'd been sent by Mr Whiteley's solicitor. People believed him: his frock coat and a silk hat helped. Anyway, he went through into Whiteley's office. Whiteley and Raynor emerged after about half an hour. Whiteley was asking for the police. Raynor pulled out a revolver from his left breast pocket and killed him. He tried to kill himself afterwards but only injured himself. They carted him off to St Mary's Hospital, where he said he was Cecil Whiteley, William's illegitimate son. Apparently William Whiteley had strongly denied it."

It's strange to think about this happening so long ago, with my great-grandfather playing a crucial, if unfortunate, role. She wants my reaction, I suppose. Something to bring the story full circle.

"What I want from you," she says (here it comes, I think), "is for you to write about your impressions of Whiteleys, armed as you are with all this history and your personal connections. I just think it will be an interesting way of exploring the subject."

I think that's fair enough, and say so. I guess some blurb from me will break up her learned observations on the locale.

"It's just as well all this didn't happen a couple of centuries earlier," she says.

"How come?"

"Well, Horace was sentenced to death after being convicted of murder. It was the first trial in the Old Bailey's new building. If it had been back in the eighteenth century, he'd probably have found himself hanging from the Tyburn tree. All that's left of it now is a round stone embedded in a traffic island where the Edgware Road meets the Bayswater Road. But it was a massive wooden triangle held up in the air by a post. Eight people could hang from each side of it."

"That's pretty gruesome."

"Yes. Anyway," she continues, "as I said on the phone, Horace was reprieved when two hundred thousand people signed a petition in protest at his sentence. He got a prison sentence instead and was released after twelve years. He disappeared after that, leaving only enough traces for me to track you down after lots of research."

The old woman next to us decides it's time to join in. She's finally made it through the meringues, apart from a few smears on her face that she's saving for later.

"I was a shop girl at Whiteleys, you know. Not when Mr Whiteley was alive, but after it was owned by Gordon Selfridge."

And they're off. The girl's much more interested in the old dear than me now. I make my excuses. Say I'm going to look at Whiteleys and I'll email later about deadlines and my fee. I leave them chatting and do a kind of urban slalom between the sticky tables to get back out into the street.

It's not much further to Whiteleys itself. It has a tall, domed tower at the corner nearest to me. Writer mode again:

There's a flag flying: red, white and blue against a moody, muddled grey. The building stretches away from the tower, a lesson in vanishing points for a student of perspective drawing. It has a slight air of crossness at being in the middle of these streets of people and small-time shops.

I go in. Good to see the place is flourishing despite great-grandfather's best efforts. Now concentrate, stop circling the issue. How am I going to write this thing up?

The coolest guy I know

Ian Marchant

Travelling west on the Tube with Steve and Marie after rehearsal one evening recently, I was visited by a sudden and painful erection, caused by the realisation that I still fancied Marie, even though we had split up over a year ago. I was a bit pissed at first when she went off with the front man, just because he's pretty and blond and talented, but I'm over it. You need to keep singers happy. She's put on a bit of weight. I guess that means she's happy with Steve too, although now I come to think of it, my sister put on weight because she was so miserable after that wanker her ex-husband dumped her. It could go either way, I guess. Perhaps Marie's weight gain is unrelated to her emotional condition.

Of course, Steve is a fucking brilliant singer, and we write fuck-off songs together, and Marie is the singer's girl now, and I wouldn't do anything to split up the band, not now we've cut back on the fist fights and seem to be getting close to something. Marie and I were miserable together, at least at the end, so my fancying her now means nothing. The Underground is a highly sexualised space, anyway. A glimpse of stockinged thigh on the Tube is sometimes worth more than a shag after a gig, in my view. Perhaps it was this and nothing more that had revived my desire for Marie, but I had to admit that a few extra pounds seem to suit her, especially on her legs, which have filled out quite spectacularly. Steve, easily the coolest guy I know, is a lucky geezer.

"Oi, are you looking at Marie's legs?" said Steve, leaning towards me across his lovely girlfriend.

"I am, actually."

"Yeah, well, fuckin' don't."

"You could write a song about my legs," said Marie. "They are very good."

"Yeah, an' I'll call it Don't Look at My Girl Friend's Legs or I'll Wrap that Fuckin' Guitar Round Your Skinny Neck."

"Can I look at her tits, then?"

"I love it when you fight over me," said Marie.

We were sitting in a row on one of those seats that run length-ways along the carriage; me with a rekindled awareness of Marie's sexual possibilities and my guitar case propped strategically between my thighs; Marie with her yummy remodeled legs; and Steve with his rockist slouch and his new haircut and his old sheepskin coat and his art-school attitude.

We pulled into Baker Street and a couple in late middle age got into the carriage and came and sat in the row opposite, a few seats down from me. They were holding hands. They looked prosperous; both had white hair and tanned skin, and they were both dressed up, him in a dark blue overcoat, her in a turquoise suit. Although the display of hand-holding seemed to indicate the man was fond of his wife, I could have sworn he was staring at Marie's born-again legs, staring really hard.

Despite sharing the old man's enthusiasm, I felt a mild distaste. There's something discomfiting about the lust of the old for the young, though I'm sure I'll feel different when I'm his age. I just thought he was being a dirty old bastard. But I was wrong; I had miscalculated the angle of his gaze, trigonometry never having been my strong point. He was staring at Steve.

"Steven?" he said, in a really posh voice.

Steve didn't move. I don't think he heard over the rattle of the train. Marie nudged him.

"Steven!" the old guy said again, louder, a sharper note in his voice.

Steve sat up straight, looked at the guy, and gulped.

"Mr Crouch!" he said.

"Steven! Hello!" The old guy turned to his wife.

"Do you remember Steven, Helen? Steven Hodson. He was head boy, what, five, six years ago?" His wife smiled and tilted her head towards us. Marie and I turned to look at Steve; he had shrunk back into the seat a little.

"Five years ago, sir," he said.

"Yes, that's right. Five years ago. There's no need for 'sir' now, is there, Helen?" His wife smiled and nodded.

"Goodness me! It's Alan now."

Steve's lips parted in a ghastly approximation of a smile.

"So, what are you up to? The last time I saw you must have been about three years ago, at an Old Boys' rugger match, or the cricket, was it? Can't quite remember. You were at Warwick?"

"Yes."

"So what are you up to now?"

"I'm doing an MA in criminology," said Steve, looking at the floor of the carriage, the smile mercifully gone.

"And singing in the best band in London," I said.

Alan and Helen looked at me as you might at talking dog shit.

"An MA?" said Alan. "Really? Hang on, we'll come and sit a little closer. Can't hear you properly."

Still holding hands, Alan and Helen shifted down the carriage so that he was opposite Steve and she was opposite Marie. Steve shrank a little further.

"An MA? In criminology, did you say?" said Alan.

"Yes si . . . Alan." Alan winced almost imperceptibly.

"Marvellous. Marvellous. Here in London?"

"Yes, sir. North London."

Alan furrowed his brow. "North London? That's one of the new ones, isn't it? Where is it?"

"Holloway Road, sir. The sociology department is very well thought of."

"Sociology?" An involuntary moue passed over Alan's lips.

"Yes, sir. My degree was in sociology."

"Oh, you gave up history?"

"Yes, sir."

"I'm sorry to hear that."

"Yes, sir."

"Ah, but do you still act?"

Steve blushed. "No. No, I don't."

"Oh, that is a shame. A great shame." Alan turned to Helen. "Do you remember seeing Steven in that production we did of *Antigone* five or six years ago?" The train was slowing now.

"Five," said Steve.

"That's right. About five years ago?"

Helen looked thoughtful. "No," she said, but when Alan looked disappointed, she added, "Oh yes . . .yes. Vaguely."

"We did *Antigone* when I was up at Cambridge, thirty or more years ago. Marvellous. I was the second soldier," said Alan.

"Was it a speaking part?" asked Helen.

"Well, I had a couple of lines, but it was very sad. Very sad." Alan shook his head and smiled broadly.

The train came to a stop in the tunnel. There was no escape.

"Of course," Alan continued, "everything was paid for in those days. The grant covered everything. Not like now, eh? We even had enough money for beer!" He laughed at memories of quaffing foaming pints of nutbrown ale by the fireside of Fenland inns long ago. Steve forced another weak smile across his pop-star lips.

"Always enough money for drink, sir," he said. Alan sobered up.

"Quite right. Quite right. So how goes the MA?"

The train lurched forward again, into the light of Edgware Road station.

"Very well, sir."

"Heading for a distinction?"

"Well, I'm borderline, sir. Between a high merit and a low distinction."

"I'm not surprised." Alan turned to his wife. "Steven was always one of the brightest of my pupils." I could feel Marie shaking with the effort of suppressing her laughter.

"Yes, very bright," said Alan. "Very promising. And a first-rate head boy."

This was too much for Marie, who went "Pah!" just as the doors luckily slid open with a "Paf!" of their own, disguising some of her pleasure. Helen peered at Marie's legs over the top of her spectacles.

"This is our stop, sir," said Steve, starting to stand up.

We stayed sitting.

"No, it isn't," said Marie. Steve sat down again.

"You haven't introduced your friends," Alan said.

"I'm sorry, sir," said Steve. "This is Marie and Robert." We smiled, and Alan and Helen smiled back with a glint of frost.

"And are you studying for your MAs too?" asked Alan.

We nodded, even though we weren't.

Alan smiled again. "You know, I remember the last time I saw you now, Steven. It wasn't at the cricket. It was on the Tube. Isn't that extraordinary?'

"Yes, sir."

"I'd been doing my Christmas shopping, that's right. I was loaded down with books and CDs . . . and books and CDs!"

Helen and Steve laughed at this little pleasantry, Helen with affectionate memory, Steve with forced politeness.

The wheels ticked over the rails. I mimicked their rhythm, whispering to Marie, "Books and CDs, books and CDs, books and CDs." Marie forced her nails into the back of my hand.

"Do you remember, Helen? That was the year when I put an empty CD case in everyone's present!"

Helen laughed. "Yes. You're expecting a really expensive present, and the first thing you see is an empty CD case." Alan laughed too, but the strain was clearly beginning to get to Steve. The smile still clung to his face, but tears were starting to well in his eyes.

"The thing was," Helen continued, "that I'd cracked one of my CD cases, and an empty one came in handy."

I sensed she was trying to make the best of things; for what, after all, was Alan's taste in CDs? Harrison Birtwistle? Hindemith? Einstürzende Neubauten? You can never tell. Perhaps an empty case signified a blessed silence in their household.

"Where are you all heading for?" said Alan.

"Bayswater," I said.

"We're going to buy drugs," said Marie.

"It's Paddington for us, of course, Steven," said Alan.

"We've been to see Richard Eyre's *Hedda Gabler* at the Almeida," said Helen.

"Have you seen it?" asked Alan.

"No, sir."

"Oh, you should. It's marvellous. We're Friends of the Almeida; we see everything. But I'm blowed if I'm going to drive into the centre of London, so we always leave the car at Marlow station, and come in on the train."

Alan and Helen stood up.

"Such a shame you didn't pursue history. You did a project on Victorian railways for GCSE, didn't you?"

"Yes, sir."

"Then I expect you'll know better than I do that Paddington was the world's first underground railway station . . . and here we are. Nice to see you again, Steven, wasn't it, Helen?"

"And to meet your friends," said Helen.

We smiled. Alan and Helen got down from the train and walked along the platform. As the train pulled past them, they waved farewell, and Steve waved back.

Steve was unusually quiet. He seemed to be intent on reading an advert for cut-price holiday insurance just above the seat where Alan had been sitting. Marie and I looked at one another.

"Steven," I said.

"What?"

"Have you got something to tell us?" said Marie.

"What?"

"You told me you went to a big inner-city comprehensive," said Marie.

"You told me you got expelled for stealing motors," I said. "You told me you got sent to a young offenders' institute."

"You told me that's why you were doing criminology," said Marie.

"Did I?" said Steve.

"Yes," I said.

Steve prepared to make a last stand.

"Well, who's to say I didn't?"

"Head boy?" said Marie.

"*Antigone*?" I said.

"*Did* you go to a large inner-city comprehensive, Steven? *Were* you in a young offenders' institute?" I asked.

"Or did you, in fact, attend a minor public school near Marlow?" said Marie.

Steve grinned. He really is very pretty.

"Yes, you bastards. And Crouch was my housemaster."

"Alan," I said. We all started screaming – with relief, I think, as much as anything. People further down the carriage turned and looked. And then the doors slid open again, and it was Bayswater, and we had business to attend to, so we said no more about it.

An Arabian Night

David Varela

It is said (though Allah knows all) that in a kingdom far to the west, between the vale of Maida and the white arch of triumph, lived a young prince by the name of Ahmed. The prince was always causing trouble and his father, the caliph, despaired of his behaviour. The caliph kept his son confined to the court, where the prince neglected his studies all day. His tutor, the vizier, was determined to teach the boy discipline, and every night he would lock Prince Ahmed in a room in the highest tower of the court.

From his room, Prince Ahmed could see a great market to the south where the people traded and revelled all night, for it was a joyous kingdom. One evening, as he watched from his window, Ahmed saw an old beggar leave the court through a secret gate. Ahmed wondered why a beggar would be in the court so late, and his wonder grew a few hours later when he saw the hooded beggar returning to the court the same way.

The next morning, Ahmed said to the vizier, "Why was there a beggar in the court last night?"

The vizier looked dumbfounded for a moment, and then replied, "There was no beggar here."

Prince Ahmed protested, but no matter how much he argued, the vizier would not change his answer.

For the next two nights, the young prince saw the beggar come and go through the secret gate; each morning, the vizier denied there was any such man. On the fourth night Prince Ahmed grew impatient, and when he saw the beggar at the gate, he shouted from his window, "You, beggar! What are you doing in my father's court?"

Surprised, the beggar turned and looked up. Greater was the prince's surprise when he saw the beggar's face: it was that of his father, the caliph!

The next morning, the young prince spoke to the vizier once more. "Why does my father go out into the market every night?"

The vizier realised that the prince could not be denied again. "Your father wishes to observe his people and ensure that they are happy."

The prince asked if he too could go out in secret to see the people. But the vizier replied, "You cannot see the market until you are a man."

Angry, the young prince cried, "I will never become a man locked up here!" and he vowed to see the market for himself.

That night, Prince Ahmed waited by his window until the clouds hid the moon. He tied his sheets together and climbed down from his window to the terrace below, creeping through the court and gardens and then out through the secret gate.

Prince Ahmed stood outside the court's walls for the first time and breathed the air. It was not as sweet as in the court, but it smelled new and wonderful to him.

Between the court and the kingdom was a crossroads with a river rising from under the earth. Prince Ahmed dipped his hands in the spring and drank from its waters. He had never tasted water so foul but so fresh! He quickly rubbed the murky water over himself and tore the gold buttons from his clothes so that he too would look like a beggar.

Pleased with his appearance, the prince walked towards the entrance of the market. There stood a huge tower, the height of twenty men, held together by a red iron scaffold. As he passed under its shadow, he saw dozens of the kingdom's citizens at its windows, hanging their washing and calling down to the street. It looked like a whole city in one building. Still, the young prince did not stop long. There was so much more to see.

So on he walked, joining the hordes in the market itself. What he saw amazed him: a thousand stalls with fruits and vegetables from every earthly kingdom. There were ripe red mangoes from Al-Jannat, pineapples from Al-Sultan, fennel from Kandoo, chicory from Hsing, carrots and potatoes from the northern lands, and scores of shrubs and seeds that the young prince had never seen before. "Surely every plant and every person in the world is here," he thought.

The crowds pushed the prince along with them, and as he walked, he grew hungry. But he had no money for food, for he had never had need of money before. The smell and the sight of the many dishes became torture to him, and soon he could stand it no more.

The prince followed the most delicious scent until it brought him to the stall of Sarchenar, the shawarma seller. He gave Sarchenar one of his gold buttons and asked for the very largest shawarma he could provide. Sarchenar looked strangely at the button, then invited the young prince to sit on a cushion while he waited. Sarchenar brought him a tall, sweet-smelling hookah that bubbled with intoxicating smoke. The prince had never smelled such smoke before, and as he waited for Sarchenar to prepare his shawarma, he tasted deeply of it and found it pleasant. He breathed in the smoke again and again until the cushion became more and more comfortable and the market seemed further and further away.

Prince Ahmed returned to his senses only when he felt rough hands dragging him to his feet, and heard Sarchenar handing him over to the market's lawmen. "This boy tried to pay me with a gold button carved with the royal seal. He must be a thief!" Before he could protest, he was hauled away and thrown into a cell. The walls of the prison were the highest and thickest of any in the kingdom, and the young prince knew he had no hope of escape. The most dangerous criminals in the land could be held for all eternity in this place without ever seeing a magistrate.

The lawmen took the gold buttons from him and divided them among themselves. "I am Prince Ahmed, son of the caliph, and I will see you punished for this impudence!" he cried, but the lawmen only laughed and spat at him through the bars of his cell. For the first time, the prince realised that he might never see his father again, and in that moment he felt lonelier than the desert.

But the prince was not alone. He heard a noise behind him and turned. "Who are you?"

"My name is Davalou and I am the most skilful thief in the kingdom. Are you truly the prince?"

Prince Ahmed said that he was, but Davalou demanded proof. "If you are the prince, tell me something that only he would know. If you can convince me, I will take you with me when I escape."

The young prince struggled to think of something only he would know. "My father the caliph creeps out of the court every night dressed as a beggar to observe his people."

But Davalou just laughed. "An old rumour! Everybody knows that story."

Even when the young prince insisted it was true, the thief would not believe him.

"I will believe you only if you can tell me how the caliph gets in and out of the court at night."

So Prince Ahmed told Davalou about the secret gate and where it could be found. Davalou nodded to himself and was satisfied. "Well, my young prince, it seems I owe you a secret of my own. Follow me."

With that, he stood up and clawed at the ground where he had sat, revealing the entrance to a long, dark passage. "This tunnel has been my secret for many months. I have been waiting for a reason to escape and now you have given it to me. Thank you."

Davalou led him down into the tunnel and through the darkness until at length they emerged from a hole in the ground outside the prison walls. Davalou bowed.

"I promise I will take from the court only what I need to live a comfortable life. Then I will leave the kingdom and your land will never be troubled by me again." With that, he turned and disappeared into the night.

The prince's mouth was full of dirt from the tunnel and he felt a terrible thirst. To his surprise, he saw a beautiful oasis right next to the prison. Tall palm trees rose above it, and elegant maidens beckoned travellers to approach. Prince Ahmed ran and threw himself down by the cool water, drinking his fill. The sand was soft and the water clear. The maidens bathed his feet and hands, washing away the smell of the prison.

The prince soon began to relax. The longer he stayed there, the less he wished to move. Such luxury and comfort surpassed even his life in the court, and he grew lazy and sluggish. But when he scooped up the water of the pool once more, he saw his reflection and noticed the heavy lids and slack mouth, and knew that he must leave. The oasis was sapping his strength and slowing his journey. There was so much more to see, and even if the rest of the market was less soothing than this heavenly place, he resolved to stay no longer.

Kissing the maidens goodbye, Prince Ahmed set off towards the market again. Before long, he came to a crossroads and saw two enormous jinns rising far above the shops and stalls. Their names were Maroush and Ranoush and they were brothers, constantly arguing and swinging their enormous clubs at each other. Because they were jinns, the clubs passed through them like knives through fire. The people of the market were not so fortunate, however, and the clubs would smash anything or anyone that stood in their way.

The people tried to carry on with their work and keep out of the jinns' reach. Prince Ahmed could glimpse the rest of the market beyond the battling monsters, but he could see no way around them.

"The food on my side of the market is more delicious than on yours!" shouted Ranoush.

"You lie," yelled Maroush. "The meat here is more succulent and the spices are more appetising."

And with that, Ranoush swung his club clean through his brother's head, blowing it away like smoke. Then Maroush returned the stroke, carving right through his brother's body from the shoulders to the feet. The club shattered the rocks where Ranoush stood, and Prince Ahmed felt the earth shudder.

"Great jinns, may Allah keep you," said the prince. "Please excuse my interruption, but I think I may be able to help."

The two jinns looked down at him, and for a moment he feared they would crush him for his impertinence. "Little man," said Ranoush, "why would we need the services of an insignificant mortal? Go about your business or we will destroy you."

"I seek only to bring you happiness, mighty jinns," replied the prince. "Perhaps if you both prepared some food for me from either side of your great market here, I could act as judge in your dispute."

Maroush stared at him. "No man has ever dared tell us what to do. Dare you face the anger of my brother when he loses?"

"I will not lose!" declared Ranoush. At once he strode across to the traders on his side of the market and commanded them to prepare the greatest feast they had ever assembled. Maroush turned to his side of the market and ordered the stall-holders to start baking and boiling and steaming and frying. The two jinns bellowed at the terrified mortals and waved their clubs, exhorting them to create the most sumptuous dishes.

Prince Ahmed knew that whichever jinn lost the contest would seek to kill him. So while the gigantic brothers roared at the unfortunate citizens, the prince ran off into the far reaches of the market until he could no longer be seen. Thus he escaped the anger of both raging brutes.

Indeed, Prince Ahmed's cunning brought him the most extraordinary spectacle. In this newfound part of the market, he discovered Al-Mustafa's fabled hall of treasures. The walls shimmered with gold plates and silver goblets while the ceiling hung heavy with diamond chandeliers. All around him were chairs and hookahs and coffeepots dripping with jacinths and pearls. Even the caliph's court held nothing to match such opulence.

In the middle of it all was the trader Al-Mustafa, surrounded by old men and women handing him their money and struggling to carry away their precious purchases. The prince sought to help an old woman with a solid-gold throne, but Al-Mustafa berated him. "Stop! Anyone may buy what they wish here, but each person must bear their load alone. That is my only rule."

Prince Ahmed looked about him and saw the greediest men faltering under the burden of their riches. As he left Al-Mustafa's hall, he felt thankful that he did not have to carry even a single gold button with him.

He noticed that the market was becoming quieter. The stalls were fewer and the sun would soon rise. The people shopping in this place were older and sicklier than elsewhere, and huddled round the tables of physicians and pharmacists, rushing to buy any unguent or powder that might bring them health.

But the prince walked on, keen to see what he would find at the end of the market.

Past all the stalls and all the shops, away from the crowds and the bartering voices, far from the vale and the court, beyond the scenes of his many adventures, Prince Ahmed found a withered tree where strange fruit had once hung. Only a shadow of the black tree remained, but the prince saw that it was a peaceful place, and weariness overcame him. His muscles ached, his joints grew stiff, and he could not walk another step.

The prince curled up at the base of the tree and closed his eyes, reflecting on his journey and all that he had seen, and wondering where his father might be. Before the prince fell asleep, the pain in his body faded away, and only then did he realise that he had long since been a man.

A strong bond with the frame

Steve Mullins

It's quite possible Simon Flatau has enough energy to power the whole of the Circle Line. Flatau is the line controller of the Metropolitan Line, Hammersmith and City Line and Circle Line at London Underground's Control Office at Baker Street, which is tucked in behind the Tube station close to Madame Tussaud's. That's where I meet him, and he walks me down to the platform to take a train over to Edgware Road.

He finds something interesting wherever we go, pointing it out with the enthusiasm of a schoolboy, albeit an exceedingly knowledgeable one, on a day trip. If he'd stayed on at school until the sixth form – he left at fifteen to work on the Tube – he'd surely have made a superb head boy.

Flatau never looks more at home than when he's in a signal cabin. And at Edgware Road, which houses some of the oldest signalling equipment on the entire London Underground system, he enthuses over what's known as the frame, a waist-high steel box topped with an array of levers used to change the signals on the stretch of line covered by the cabin. Here, the signalman on duty – eight-hour shifts with half-hour meal relief and two breaks for "personal needs" – tends trains travelling between Baker Street and Paddington.

Traffic movements are shown on a five-foot-wide illuminated diagram dating back eighty years or so, and also on a more recent monitor. For look and feel, the old display wins hands down; the electronic device is a must- rather than a wanna-have.

"This is where a signal operator learns the basics, serves an apprenticeship," Flatau says. "And it takes years to get the knowledge. Experience is a culmination of many a good fuck-up."

The operator working the Edgware Road frame has to step back to lift a radio from a wall rack, and another signalman steps in ready to take over. I ask myself what it might be like to have responsibility for so much train tonnage and its human freight. Absolutely terrifying.

Flatau knows what's on my mind. "See," he says. "No hesitation. He just walked right in there. You have a strong bond with the frame. And it would be second nature to me as well. A natural thing."

I see he's eager to jump in, exercise an old skill, check if the muscle memory will kick in.

On joining the Tube in 1981, Flatau trained on signals, and after two years moved on to lift operations at Elephant & Castle. "I wanted to work in a signals cabin, but on the Underground it's seniority that counts, and you have to wait your turn until there's a vacancy."

After the Elephant, he found himself cleaning the toilets at Piccadilly Circus – "Awful, all those needles" – and trimming the wicks of the oil lamps that used to ride on the back of Bakerloo Line trains until the mid 1980s. He got his hands back on a frame in the Hammersmith cabin with its mile of signalling, before moving on to West Ruislip and then Edgware Road, each time skipping up through the grades. (Cabins are graded on the degree of complexity and responsibility associated with their track.)

"Look at the workmanship in that door and window frame," he tells me as we stand behind the signal operators in the Edgware cabin. He's right. It's beautiful. Hardwood panels and surrounds, small panes of glass framed with copper strip.

"I wish I had a house where I could put that, whenever they take it out," he says. "It's fantastic."

We wait for a train to take us a stop back to Baker Street. When it arrives, there's a change of drivers and the next operator makes his way up from the platform, bag over his shoulder, in no particular hurry. "He should have been here already." Flatau shakes his head. Maybe he's thinking of the signals operators we've left back in the cabin, how they're looking at the train failing to move away on a green light; maybe they're as disappointed as he is.

"Are you a signalman?" I ask. It seems the obvious question. Signalling must be in his blood.

"No, I'm a railwayman. And I'll do anything to make the Underground run well. It's pride."

Flatau tells the driver he's the line controller and gets a look of indifference. He asks if we can ride up front to the next station. This time he gets a nod. In the cab, as we disappear into the dark of a tunnel, I ask Flatau if he's ever driven a train.

"Yes. But if I were doing it now we'd be going a lot slower. I'd be worried about going too fast. I wouldn't be as comfortable as he is."

Outside the door to the Signalling Control Centre at Baker Street, Flatau is telling me how he landed his present job. In 1988, he began working on the implementation of computer-based signalling at Neasden, assisting in the proofreading and test-driving of the new rule book associated with the project. He really enjoyed it, he says, and ended up going back to school part-time to take a Chartered Institute of Transport degree at University College Harrow in London. He graduated in 1998. Two years after that, he was promoted to line controller, and he felt he'd made it.

"My father was a Royal Navy man and he made captain," he says. "And here I was, captain of my ship, so to speak. It was good to be able to look him in the eye and say 'Now I've achieved what you've achieved.'"

The Signalling Control Centre reminds me of the bridge on the Starship *Enterprise*. A couple of assistants sit at the monitoring station and keep an eye on the fixed-line diagram: a long analogue display that looks not unlike an illuminated version of the familiar Underground map. Trains are represented by blocks of red light that travel along the network, stop at stations and negotiate points and bends. It's a Hornby enthusiast's dream. The assistants also watch computer screens showing graphic representations of sections of the network that they can slide into view using a tracker ball. I prefer the fixed-line diagram; it's closer to the romantic image I had before I came here.

The staff here oversee the stretch of the Circle Line that runs from Aldgate to Baker Street; the remaining track is the responsibility of the control centre at Earl's Court. Despite the impression created by the neat yellow circuit on the Tube map, the Circle Line barely exists as an autonomous piece of infrastructure. There may be 27 stations and 22.5 kilometres of track, but for more than 95 percent of its journey a Circle Line train is actually piggybacking off District Line and Hammersmith and City Line hardware. There are only two lengths of track dedicated exclusively to the Circle Line. (For Tube purists, these are the less than a kilometre stretch from High Street Kensington to Gloucester Road, and the tiny leg from Aldgate to Tower Hill.)

Computers pretty much run the show, but the assistants are able to intervene and tell them what to do if necessary. They react to arrowed messages at the top of their screens and pull up what's known as an edit that can hold a train in a given place, or simply cancel it. Flatau glances at the fixed-line diagram. "You watch the board for headways, which is the time between the back of one train and the front of the next. The job's about balancing headways, avoiding the bunching of trains and inconveniencing as few people as possible. The assistants adjust and regulate headways."

Trains on the Circle Line generally run every eight minutes and alternate with Metropolitan Line stock on the north side and District Line trains on the south side. There's a timetable – the first train of the day leaves Aldgate at 4.42 a.m. – but I've already done a lap of the Circle Line with an experienced driver who never once looked at his watch. He said he didn't need to; he just knew by the way he was running whether he was on time or not.

On that trip, I travelled eastward in the cab out of Edgware Road on the part of the track known as the outer. The outer takes about an hour to circumnavigate; the inner is two minutes faster. Drivers are attuned to the difference and prefer the inner. They're usually required to do three consecutive circuits on a shift, and say it's tougher than working on a linear route, where they get a break from driving when they reach their destination and have to walk the length of the train to switch cabs.

At the Signalling Control Centre, the assistants seem incredibly relaxed considering they have the responsibility for so many people's lives. At rush hour, when the cars are full to capacity (what's known as crush loading), there can be as many as a thousand passengers on a single train. The assistants calmly look from the diagram to the monitors, make and take phone calls, tap on the keyboards now and again and chat. "Recruitment comes largely from the signalling side," Flatau tells me. "An assistant needs to know what the mechanical system's doing. They're handpicked and have to take a railway-oriented IQ test."

He says everyone knows the protocol when a problem arises. "It's an experience thing. A signal failure at Aldgate might mean a forty-minute delay, whereas elsewhere it might be just five minutes." I talk about the timetable again, about how the whole job must revolve around keeping everything as punctual as possible. "The one thing trains don't do is run early, and it's the signals that stop them," Flatau says. "As far as we're concerned, a train is always late until it's on time."

The Circle Line boasts 14 trains for most of the day, down to 12 in the late evening. But there's recourse to additional stock, and trains can be pulled out of service elsewhere if the need arises. "You can, for example, steal a Wimbledon train from the District Line and use it on the Circle Line," Flatau explains. It sounds like a puzzle, some kind of pacy multidimensional board game. "As a controller," Flatau says, "I know where a train is, where it will be, how it slots in. It's a matter of distance, speed and time, that's all."

But, I point out, it's not a closed system. There are unpredictable passengers to deal with, and a good deal of the track is overground and open to the elements. He nods. "You can have problems with the weather, such as ice and snow between Farringdon and King's Cross." Plus there are rats and mice on the tracks, I say. "And pigeons. Dogs are a pain because any death has to be reported to the police. But cats are classed as domesticated vermin. And there have been foxes and swans, and badgers outside central London."

There's more than livestock stalking the rails. In Tube parlance, an incident involving a person hit by a train is a "one-under." "There's an average of a person a week on the tracks, and two a week at the beginning and end of the year," Flatau says. "In December, it's perhaps because someone's run off with the Christmas money, I don't know; and in January, it's probably post-Christmas depression." After a clean-cut one-under, trains might be up and running again in just forty minutes, whereas something more complicated might stop the trains for twice as long.

"Clean-cut" means that any bodily injury has been cut and sealed by the pressure of the wheels and the heat of the rail. The doctor will quickly certify death (every station has a body bag at the ready), and the police will question the driver and look at the CCTV recording. If everything matches up, the driver takes the train away. "The driver who was up there when the one-under happened?" I ask. "We prefer it that way," says Flatau. "It's like when you fall off your bike and graze your knee, and your dad tells you to get back on."

Drivers can take time off and get counselling for a one-under. They are trained to react immediately: sit back, cross their arms and close their eyes. The train automatically comes to a halt when the dead man's handle is released. But the forty-minute rule goes out of the window if there is anything at all suspicious about the incident. "If it's a crime scene – if someone was pushed or tripped or lost their balance – then we lose control of the event," Flatau says.

Though the Circle Line is a loop, one blockage doesn't necessarily shut down the whole circuit. Trains can be turned around and sent back at certain points in the network, so there's almost always some kind of limited service in operation. With a complicated one-under, the Emergency Response Unit is called in. Its special tenders are equipped with heavy lifting gear, block and tackle, props, breathing apparatus and the like. "It's rare the team will cut anyone out," Flatau explains. "They'll dismantle the train to remove a body. There can be a lot of gore, but they're specially trained."

Cleaning up can be quick: the fire service can come down with high-pressure hoses and trains can be taken away for washing. However, Flatau tells of one incident in Uxbridge where the station staff spent hours looking for a missing limb before they found out that the one-under was a war veteran with one arm. At this stage, I get the sense that Flatau's seen it all, that whatever happens, he and his team will deal with it imperturbably. He looks around the Signalling Control Centre, still the picture of calm. "If there's an incident, we always ask ourselves 'Can we work around it?'" he says.

Something cooking

Stuart Delves

I dream of an imaginary Underground, based on the incalculable strangeness of the first time, aged seven, that I saw the London Tube on a school trip.

Michael Bywater, broadcaster, cook, harpsichordist and pilot, in *Lost Worlds*

Imagination is more important than knowledge. Knowledge is limited. Imagination encircles the world.

Albert Einstein, patent-office clerk, physicist, theorist and genius

Baker Street. It's one of the first Tube stations, its original caverns a gas-lit oasis off the yowling 1863 Metropolitan, the world's pioneering underground line. Today it's the nexus of five lines. Only the mighty King's Cross has more arteries running through it. But then the junction of the old pastry chef has a whole line named after it, or partially named after it, thanks to Quex, the *Evening News* diarist who, in 1906, coined the name Bakerloo much to the disgust of the rail company's shareholders. Victoria, Piccadilly and Hammersmith also have lines named after them, as indeed does Waterloo, the Baker's apron-tail south of the river. But the combination of eponym and steel-road heart makes it pretty important, with 69,000 passengers passing through it every weekday.

Why, though, this intersection here? For above ground, it's a relatively recent metropolitan hub. When the Barley Mow, the oldest pub in Marylebone, was built in 1791, there were, as the name suggests, fields where the Planetarium and Madame Tussaud's now stand. Maybe it was this expanse of virgin land so close to the city's heart. Though it's hard to imagine, as you down a pint of London Pride in the pawnbroker-cum-lovers' snug with the bustle and rush palpable beyond the frosted glass.

Meet me there, 8 Dorset Street. Imagine the great sleuth, pipe packed and crackling, gazing on the gin-tap behind the bar and wondering at the state of the girt city's underbelly, hidden to his well-heeled clients making their way by coach to nearby Regent's Park. Just as today the Polish masseuse is hidden to the stream of tourists who pass blithely by the plaques to Arnold Bennett and H. G. Wells as they make their way to 221B. Strange that the carpetbaggers of Elvis and the Beatles should set up shop opposite the fictional hero of another era. But not so strange, maybe, that students and the night-bright crowd should find this a dull environ. Salubrious. Residential. And a squeaky clean station. Come in the daylight, with a glass, or the apparatus of forensics, and look again at the sprinkling of clues.

As soon as I heard of the Circle Line project – sitting in a beer tent in Edinburgh's Charlotte Square – I bagged Baker Street. Not because when I was young a tune of that title swirled off the turntable. Not even because Edinburgh is the birthplace and medical stamping-ground of Sherlock's creator. No. But because my mother worked here for a while, at 82 Michael House, the then new headquarters of Marks & Spencer. I don't know what floor she worked on. Or exactly what she worked at. Today it's a faceless office block. M&S have headed off to Paddington. But then, in 1942, beyond the racks of trousers and skirts and trestles of shirts, pyjamas and cardigans, through a door and up a stair, was the HQ of SOE, Special Operations Executive. In fact, whole blocks of Baker Street and many houses in the streets off it were occupied by British signallers and code-breakers and freedom fighters from Nazi-occupied countries such as France, Greece, Yugoslavia and Poland.

Baker Street was synonymous with SOE just as Broadway was with SIS (Secret Intelligence Service), its forerunner, rival, survivor and devourer (it mopped up many disbanded operatives after the war). The SOE staff who worked there, south of the Marylebone Road, were known as the Baker Street Irregulars. Their efforts were geared to directing, supporting and communicating with agents who were dropped into occupied Europe and South-east Asia. And *their* efforts? To cause maximum damage behind enemy lines.

This is why the organisation riled SIS, whose style was, and is, invisible infiltration and the steady accumulation of intelligence. SOE were the fireworks boys and girls. They had notable successes: blowing up the Gorgopotamos rail bridge in Greece to delay reinforcements reaching Rommel in North Africa; melding resisting factions in Yugoslavia; setting back Nazi progress in developing the atom bomb by destroying the heavy water supply at the Norsk hydro plant in southern Norway in 1943 (as recounted in *The Heroes of Telemark*); and focusing resistance and hindering enemy supply lines and thereby easing the Allied invasion of France in 1944. It's said that SOE knocked six months or more off the duration of the war. The price, for many of the agents, was heavy: torture, concentration camp or a bullet in the head. When the game was up, some understandably chose to bite through the rubber of the standard-issue three-second cyanide pill.

Who would have thought it, breezing down Baker Street today? History is, after all, the subject we seem to have most difficulty learning from. But it's all there: the fact that occupation is intolerable, whatever the grandiose reasons proclaimed by the occupier, and that the dirty tricks of warfare and subterfuge are always learnt by the enemy (whoever it is) sooner or later.

I thought this project would offer me the opportunity to do some research into the Baker Street of SOE and maybe find out what my mother did there. Did she decipher? If so, what? I do know that under cover of the First Aid Nursing Yeomanry she left Baker Street and sailed from the Clyde to Inter-Service Signal Unit No. 6 (code name Massingham) in Algiers. There she met my father, also in SOE. He was an instructor who, among other things, used his lifelong acquaintance with the French to teach agents how to pass themselves off as French by the way they ate soup or held a cigarette. Never was the devil more in the detail: survival depended on it. So I knew something of what he did then, and later in the SIS, but not what she did. Except that, as family lore had it, she was the better shot. The truth is lost, for I cannot ask her.

But when I caught up with David Stafford, project director at Edinburgh University's Centre for Second World Studies, and quizzed him about his specialities, SOE and intelligence, over a tagine in a south-side restaurant, he came up with a wild hypothesis. In all those years after 1946, when to all intents and purposes she played dutiful wife at endless embassy functions, maybe my mother (quiet, unassuming, observant, interested and attentive) was in fact the perfect foil to my father (mine host, mixing, shaking, stirring, florid, provocative, outrageous with his uncanny reading of women's palms and *pièce de resistance* of crystal-glass gazing). In other words, maybe she was the boss. His controller. Paid by HM Government. That had me chortling.

And it fits the Baker Street theme, where all is not as it seems. But I was no closer to discovery, and deadlines have so far prevented me from trawling newly released archives at Kew. Try another day. Besides, serendipity raised its downy head and flashed its merry eyes. On 25 January I flew down to London and made my way from King's Cross down to Elephant and Castle. If you look at that internationally acclaimed triumph of graphic design – Harry Beck's map of the Tube – you will see that, unless there were other errands or ports of call to divert the traveller, the most direct route would be via the Northern Line. My objective was as unwavering as Orpheus's in seeking Eurydice. I whistled past Angel and (graphically at least) intersected the Circle at Moorgate and Monument on my way to the London College of Communication (formerly Printing) where, incidentally, Beck went to teach after he left the employ of London Underground.

Elephant and Castle is also at the tail-end of the Bakerloo, being added a year later in 1907, and, as far as I can judge from the state of it in 2005, not scrubbed since. The subway system that leads from the station to the college is itself a maze, built post-Beck who, having made sense of one of the world's most enormous labyrinths, would surely have scribbled some form of linear clue. Anyway, what I found, courtesy of my young design collaborators, was a great piece of information: Baker Street, as anyone will know who has mislaid a watch, a glove, a camera or a false leg on London Transport, is the site of the lost-property office, no. 200.

I was entranced. Somehow this sparked my imagination. And it seemed so appropriate. Baker Street is a big intersection, and a lot of London Underground's offices, including recruitment, used to be sited here. But the prosaic simply underscores the thematic: Baker Street is all about hidden worlds, secret worlds, lost worlds, infinite worlds; clues, trails, codes; making connections. For me, the lost-property office provided the key to this imaginative journey. And the list I was handed over the counter the next day was like a sculptor's or painter's *objet trouvé*.

This is what I learnt: during the 12 months ending 31 March 2004, 131,148 items of lost property were handed in, including:

7,026 umbrellas
14, 112 handbags and purses
5,718 cameras, laptops and computers
2,671 pairs of gloves
474 single gloves
6,118 spectacles
20,846 books
(including cheque books and credit cards)
24,084 cases and bags
19,583 articles of clothing
7,505 keys
10,614 mobile phones
12,094 miscellaneous
303 perishables

And this is the list of unusual items that have been received at the office (over what period was not specified):

False teeth
False eyes
False limbs
Lawn mower
Chinese typewriter
Breast implants
4ft teddy bear
Theatrical coffin
Wheelchairs
Crutches
Stuffed eagle
14ft boat

Divan bed
Outboard motor
Water skis
Park bench
Grandfather clock
Bishop's crook
Garden slide
Inflatable doll
Jar of bull's sperm
Urn of ashes
Gas mask
Tibetan bell
Stuffed puffa fish
Vasectomy kit
Harpoon
Two human skulls in a bag

Oh, and a press cutting in the front office mentioned the taking into care of a burglar's kit. What an emporium of detritus and unaccountable amnesia. Stranger than fiction. In fact, downright unbelievable. But also, what a double whammy. First, the list itself, a superb roll-call of the unexpected and the mind-boggling. And second, on the heels of the boggling, the questions, the surmising, the scenarios. A field day for Holmes. Elementary? I'm not sure. Could the Chinese typewriter be a red herring? Or a sudden act of denial by the soas Maoist heading for Russell Square? Was the park bench left after a lovers' tiff? The coffin after two renegade actors agreed the script was crap? The gas mask by a terrorist with a sudden change of heart? The skulls by an anthropologist teetering on the cusp of cannibalism? The crutches by an illuminatus? Ditto the wheelchair?

What if several of these items (if not all) were found abandoned on the same train? Imagine a siren on the platform, hermaphroditic, smitingly beautiful, bathed in light, gesturing to midnight's motley crew to leave behind life's peccadilloes, then leading them upwards, through descants and escalations of joy? Maybe only the bishop hung on for a stop or two, closeting the vasectomy kit and jar of bull's sperm. We shouldn't assume he abandoned the crook. We must tread carefully and be wary of assumptions. (I'm reminded of the brilliant 1980s recruitment ad for the

Metropolitan Police that was splashed all over the Underground and confronted a raft of assumptions. In Don McCullin's photograph, it looks as though a policeman is chasing a black man, but, as Indra Sinha's copy explains, the black man is a Met plain-clothes officer and they're both chasing a third party, the real crook, off frame.)

Below, dear reader, is an interactive space (or game zone) in which to write your own scenario inspired by the list.

While we're talking of no. 200 and of what's lost, what about the Tube itself? What parts of its huge sprawling entity are dark and silent, or catch only a flicker of light or the muffled rumble of passing carriages? Limbs, real enough, heavy with plaster and iron, immovable, buried. There are forty-odd stations that for one reason or another have become surplus to requirements. King William Street, opened in 1890, closed in 1933, used in the war as an air-raid shelter, whose 1940s posters still survive; Down Street, another station that enjoyed a Blitz revival, whose relics include an old telephone exchange and Churchill's bath; North End, at 60 metres the deepest station of all, never finished, never even opened for business, but adopted in the Cold War as a control centre for activating the Underground's floodgates in the event of a nuclear attack. Someone should add to Beck's map a faded legend, half-traced roots and branches, or shimmering ghost stations, disused tunnels, abandoned sidings, forgotten platforms. And of course there's Aldwych, that anomalous spur, closed in 1994, when the £3 to £5 million cost of refurbishing the lift machinery could not be justified for a daily throughput of 600 passengers. Today it's the haunt of film crews and, as virtually every teenager knows, Lara Croft.

For me, that's by the by. This was the station that I emerged from as a fifteen-year-old boy to see Peter Brook's *A Midsummer Night's Dream* with Alan Howard as Theseus/Oberon and Sara Kestelman as Hippolyta/Titania. Nineteen seventy-one: when for me the world was so much more mysterious and full of promise, a time before so much was lost – like innocence, loon pants, parents, contemporaries. And that play . . . well, what can I say but when I left, the blood in every vein of my body seemed on fire; joy circled my throat.

I wasn't the only one. Not by a thousand or more. Critic Bernard Levin singled out one girl from the audience as they streamed excitedly out of the theatre. "She was, I would judge, about 18. She was wearing the full uniform, hot pants and all. She was bright and alive, and walked as though she owned the earth, as I suppose she did. She turned to her friend. 'It makes you want to jump up and down with happiness,' she said." Snap. All is not lost. In fact, some days – and I'm sure you'll agree – it seems just like we're found. But who was that girl? Where is she now? What lines has she followed, what diversions made? Is it simply a matter of making the right connection? Who knows who or what will show up at Baker Street?

GREAT PORTLAND STREET

In the making

Richard Owsley

In the mid-nineteenth century, blight devastated Ireland's potato crop, and famine followed. Between 1845 and 1849, over a million Irish people died, and more than a million and a half emigrated. Many thousands found work on the new railways being built all over Britain. They were known as navvies, or navigators.

A rough hand shook Davey awake. C'mon. Work. So said the voice at the end of it. Hell. Monday? He tried to gather his thoughts, without much success. Ireland, his ma, his uncles. All ran through his mind. He couldn't ever forget them. But no. This was London, he knew that much. And the work? He'd only just finished. Or so it seemed. On Saturday night. Digging ditches for the railway along New Road. Was it already time for more? The way he felt told him how the time had passed sure enough. Wrecked on the drink. Shite. And shite again.

But the gangmaster had paid them in the alehouse. They often did that. Probably something extra in it for the conniving bastards. The gangmasters ruled the roost when it came to who got paid. And when, and where. Davey began to remember more. Stepping in between two young bucks fighting. Stupid kids. What did they know? Not like the Davey of old, though. Used to be him starting the scraps. A sly grin as he recalled. Mind, there was usually a fight of sorts every night at the alehouse. He felt around for bumps and scrapes. Nothing much. Just the usual cuts and mess of the week's work. And thankfully a coin or two still to show for it. And his tin ticket. Which meant they still wanted him on the job.

So now, up and back to the digging. Hard work it was too, and dangerous. On some railway jobs you'd more chance of getting badly hurt than the men who'd fought at Waterloo, so they said. But it was a better place to be than this hovel – nothing but a cold, damp cellar under an old house. Eighteen men supposed to sleep on one muddy floor. And you couldn't even stand up. In this pit you did nothing but cough. At least there was air out on the work. Some days a bit of sunshine.

Shite though, he hated himself. How many years had he been at this railway work? It wasn't so bad. But it was just dig, drink, fight. Dig, drink, fight. Dig, drink and fight again. Till one day you just gave up. And what happened to those fellers then? You'd see them for a bit, but they'd be a real mess. And then dead, soon forgotten.

He wanted a bit more than that, did Davey. Some fellers didn't seem to. But he did. He knew there was a way out. He'd seen some do it. Working just a bit harder and being just a bit older. That was what did it. Someone would spot it. Then there'd be a bit more money and, sure, a bit more minding after the other fellers' work. So you lost a pal or two on the way, but you could get someplace. There was a way. And he was one of the older ones now.

They trudged along New Road to get back to the digging. Davey was figuring again. Trying to work out how old he was. Well, he was ten or eleven or twelve when he first came here. Skinnier by far than the London kids. A bit wiser though. There'd been a fight or two had proved that. And how many years had passed since? Ten, maybe? Less, maybe?

He gave up figuring and thought of home. He always did when he'd been on the drink. It was still home, Ireland. Though he'd had perhaps half his life digging English railways. Everyone he knew was from Ireland, too. He thought of his ma. The way she used to play with his hair. And the way she whupped him, mind. Was she alive still? Sure, his uncles wouldn't have let her come to harm. No way. They'd have fed her. Somehow. Would he see her again? He tried to think of something else. His brothers, his cousins. Where did they go? Did they find America? And what about Fergal, with his grand ideas about Argentina, wherever in hell that was? He was too clever, Fergal. By far.

But at home there was no food. No potatoes, no work, no nothing. Nothing to stay for. You had to go. Over here at least there was the railway work. And no end of it either. If you didn't work this railway you could work that railway. And if you fell out with one gang boss you'd go work for another. There were railways going up everywhere, it seemed. And even going down. Hah. Like down here amongst the shite.

By the 1840s, congestion in London was getting out of control as more and more people moved to the capital for work. With the astonishing growth of the railways, many lines served London, but they terminated on the edge of the city, where they could go no further. Support grew for an underground railway to link the main stations, and in 1854 Parliament passed an act to allow its construction. One of the greatest champions of this new idea was Charles Pearson, solicitor to the City of London, who believed it would allow the capital's workforce to move out to healthier lives in the suburbs.

Davey's gang was working on New Road. Or rather, digging up New Road. It was bollock-breaking work. But this railway was different. They were going to run it underground, all the way across London, from the edge to the middle. That was a lot of digging. Paddington Road to Farringdon Street, he'd heard. Would be one of the wonders of the world, the City gent had told them; an engineering feat the envy of every civilised nation.

Stupid auld git, Davey thought. All that money. The finest clothes. Best tobacco. A proper schooling, no doubt. And yet stupid. Who were these people? Where did they get their ideas from? All the digging, the injuries, the deaths, the chaos. Digging up the streets just so trains could run underground. Why? And what about all the smoke? Where'd that go? Hadn't they thought of that? Still, it was money, and there was precious little of that in Ireland – and none in the workhouse.

So every morning at daybreak it was off to New Road. They were digging a trench. Twenty feet down. Maybe 40 feet across. Pick, shovel and barrow were the tools. It wasn't just digging up the road either. Lots of old houses came down. Lord knows where those poor folk went to live. It was clear to Davey they had nowhere to go.

The gang was working where New Road met Portland Road now. It was going to be a stop for the trains. For the park, Davey supposed. He knew the park. The Regent's Park they called it now. His workmates wouldn't even have known it was there, though it was barely a stone's throw. Molly had shown it to him. He met Molly some Sundays. She was Irish, too. Fourteen or fifteen years old. In service at one of the big houses. He could talk to her. They talked and talked about all sorts for as long as they could before she had to return to the house. It was since he'd known Molly that he wanted to get out of the digging. To do something. He didn't know what, just something. Something with Molly. Something that wasn't dig, drink, fight; dig, drink, fight. They didn't talk about it. But he knew she was the reason he was thinking these things.

But hard work was all Davey knew. Digging and the like. He wanted to be living like the skilled men he met: smithies and riveters when the track went down, carpenters and bricklayers when the walls went up. They bricked an arch over the top after that. But Davey and his mates had their skills too. Some of these fellers would run a mile from shoring up the sides when the rain was coming down, or crowbarring the overhangs into the cutting. That was proper hard work. With a lot of accidents, too. Men broke bones, got crushed, died sometimes. But Davey liked the skilled men on the work. He wanted to learn from them. He did a good job for them. They were his way out. He knew where his future lay.

They found Davey's body one morning. Cold. Still. Bloody. Barely recognisable. Chewed up in the darkness by one of the carts they shovelled the mud into. It must have slipped its anchorage and rolled along the rail. He'd probably not have heard it until it was almost on top of him. The young boy who'd found him couldn't stop blubbing. Davey had wanted to work on a bit after the others the night before. Who knew his reason; maybe he was doing a task for one of the craftsmen, or looking for a favour from the gang boss?

They buried Davey not long after. Just a hole in the ground, an unmarked grave. The man from the railway company said a few words. His customary few words. Brave, hard worker . . . legacy for generations to come . . . fine example to the world . . . engineering that built the British Empire. Davey's mates looked on sullenly, huddled against the breeze, eyeing each other impassively. They'd heard it all before. They'd hear it all again. Unless it was them in the hole next time. They'd sink a few for Davey tonight. Word would get to his kin. His kin here in England anyways. The man was drawing his short speech to a close. In no time they'd be back digging. Back in a cold, muddy ditch, wielding their picks and breaking their backs.

Nobody noticed the servant girl standing by a tree. She had no right to be away from her duties at this time of day. Tears streaming down her face, Molly wondered if Davey had known what she knew. She had a feeling he had. Either way, it didn't matter. One thing was certain. She was now the only person in the world who knew she was carrying Davey's child.

The Metropolitan Railway Company opened for business on 10 January 1863. It was the world's first underground railway, and an immediate success, carrying 38,000 passengers on its first day.

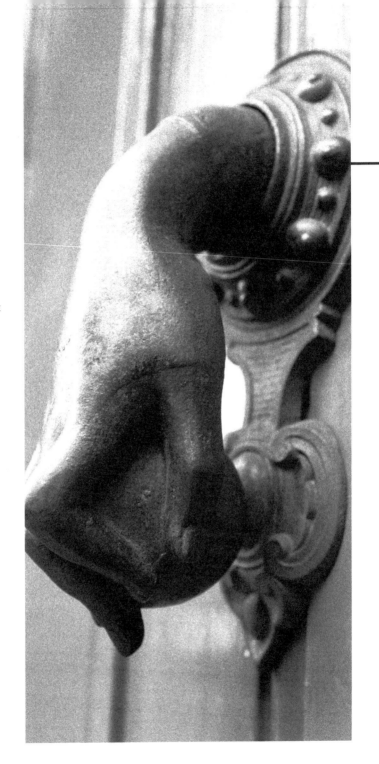

Hair of the dog

Jim Davies

Algy sat up with a start. He wasn't quite sure where he was, but he had a nagging feeling that not all was quite as it should be. His dreams – what he could remember of them – had certainly been chock full of anxiety. There'd been all the snakes of course, and at one point he recalled rowing down the River Thames on a naked woman passing herself off as a boat.

He tried opening his eyes, but they felt as if they'd been welded together. There seemed to be a construction team working inside his head, with the chap on the pneumatic drill putting in a spot of overtime. As he gradually hove into consciousness, he became aware of several not altogether pleasant tingling sensations. His right buttock was particularly tender, and his back felt as though he'd been set upon by an over-zealous sous-chef wielding a cheese-grater.

Finally, he persuaded his reluctant eyes to open a fraction, but quickly shut them again. His heart would have been in his mouth, but his tongue was as dry as a camel's, so it retreated from whence it came.

"Good God," he thought.

The thickness of Algy's eyelids offered only temporary solace from the carnage before him. He knew that sooner or later he'd have to face the music. So he slowly counted to three, and took the plunge into the sordid waters before him. As he blinkingly scanned the room, he broke into a copious, spring-loaded sweat. His formerly slicked-back, brilliantined hair stood up on end like a porcupine in a stiff breeze.

"It's one of those paintings by that Bosch fellow," he thought to himself. "Only there are more breasts and the spikes are far pointier."

The montage of tangled limbs and flesh sandwiches he gazed upon was indeed far from picturesque. Virtually every item of furniture and square inch of carpet was draped in the sorry remnants of some manner of depravity. No matter how often Algy did the maths (though admittedly this wasn't his strong suit), he still couldn't arrive at the infinite number of sexual permutations on display. Nor could he work out where one intimate cluster ended and the next began. Perhaps he was witness to the remains of a long conjoined Conga line, in which everyone's parts had a part to play.

The various, curious and dangerous accoutrements scattered about the place boggled the mind. Most appeared to have been purloined from a stables yard, while in other sections of the room, the theme was distinctly piratical.

The air – what little there was left of it – was perfumed by a heady blend of booze and nicotine, with a top note of stale sex. As far as he could tell, Algy was sharing a brass bed with a pair of voluptuous intertwined women who'd have passed muster on the Rubens casting couch, and a fully uniformed sea captain with a passing resemblance to George V.

Algy's daymare was punctured by a dissolute-looking parrot in an ornate white cage. It spewed forth a litany of moans, groans, obscenities and squawks of delight, punctuated every so often by a strange thwacking sound. Along with the discordant chorus of snores, an insistent, rhythmic rustling could be heard. There, among the endless dunes of skin and discarded clothing, a single white arse bobbed metronomically up and down, sticking to its task with inconceivable stamina.

"How in hell's name did I end up here?" wondered Algy.

The Haywain, a well-appointed gentleman's club just behind Piccadilly, was a welcome home from home for country types who'd come up to the Smoke. Townies hankering for some ridiculously romantic rustic idyll spent time there too, unwinding in the rump-sculpted leather arm-chairs, losing themselves in timeless etchings of pastoral meadows and hunting scenes, warming their credentials in front of crackling log fires.

The club's management had come up with a delightful scam. In keeping with their rural motif, they'd struck a deal with a Somerset farmer to provide them with regular barrels of Olde Doggerel Scrumpy. It was as rough as a circus roustabout, but they marked it up ten-fold and sold it with all the trappings of the finest champagne. "Doggers" was the talk of the town, even though people could barely speak after a few delicate flutes of the stuff.

Algy's morning train journey from Warwickshire had been uneventful. He dropped his bags off at the Haywain, and strode off towards Coutts, to attend to some small matter on behalf of his great-uncle Jasper. After a light luncheon at Jenner's washed down with a couple of glasses of Porter, he ambled happily around the National Gallery, and lost himself for a few delicious hours among the old masters. Though he'd never fully embraced the academic life, Algy had always been partial to classical art, a passion he indulged whenever he could.

He returned to his club around fiveish, with plenty of time for a spruce up before meeting cousin Sidney for early-evening drinks in the oak-panelled smoking room. Sidney was from the rather more urbane, London branch of the family, and ever since they were nippers, Algy had looked upon him as something of the dashing man about town. In reality he was more Debenhams than debonair, but Sidney wasn't inclined to disabuse his country cousin.

Sidney was on tip-top form. In fact, Algy had the distinct impression that he'd stopped off for some earlier early-evening drinks en route. And by the time he'd downed three Doggers, Algy could tell that his pink-cheeked cousin meant to make a night of it.

"Look… tell you what," said Sidney with a slur of excitement. "Why don't we head over to the Warren at Euston Square? You'd absolutely love it… love it. Arty-farty types… you know."

Algy didn't exactly, but the name rang distant bells and, his curiosity tickled, he agreed.

Of late, Euston Square and its environs had developed a less-than-upstanding reputation. It had become a magnet for raffish divorcees, indolent students, uppity northerners, anarchic artists and non-conformist intellectuals. Shunned by "proper society," it nevertheless had a certain seductive, Bohemian charm. Just about everyone and everything were tolerated – which was probably just as well. Euston Square was on the cusp of Bloomsbury, slightly frowned upon by the more respectable Gordon, Brunswick and Fitzroy Squares, but wallowing in its glorious moment of notoriety.

The place was positively bristling with brainpower and all manner of cultural goings-on. The indefatigable Charles Dickens had lodged just around the corner. A stone's throw away at University College London, the mummified remains of the radical idealist Jeremy Bentham kept a dull eye on academic proceedings from a wooden cabinet. Yet more whiffy relics had a home in the nearby British Museum, while in the circular Reading Room, influential chaps scratched their impressive bonces and scribbled away at books and treatises that would make them even more influential.

You could tell the neighbourhood was elbowing its way into history – just a few months ago, the local Tube station had changed its name from Gower Street to Euston Square. Quite so. After all, you could argue that this was the birthplace of modern transport. In 1808, much to the consternation of the terrified local populace, Cornishman Richard Trevithick, the father of the steam engine, showed off his prototype Catch Me Who Can locomotive. It ran in toy-like circles at 12mph around a track behind a tall fence in Euston Square.

On the cab in the way over, Sidney did his best to give his ingenuous cousin the low-down, though by now constructing a sentence had become a challenge.

"The Warren's just a group... circle... or maze rather... of people who get together every so often for a bit of a chinwag," he explained, slowly and deliberately. "The conversation always touches exceptionally high levels of brilliance, of course, but you get to meet some interesting types... different, I suppose, you'd call them. I've yet to come across Warren himself though."

They pulled up in front of an imposing three-storey Georgian building. On the corner of the square, a vendor selling the *Evening News* bellowed something approximating "Eeee-nooooo!". The rudimentary poster flapping on his stand read "WG Grace plays final innings".

"Actually, change of plan… bit queasy… something I ate," said Sidney, his head wobbling slightly. "Think I'll take the cab home. But go on old boy… you'll have a ball."

So Algy got out, saw his cousin off, and tentatively knocked on the door. He was greeted by a large man in a loud pin-stripe suit and a fez. The colossus said nothing, but smiled exaggeratedly and, with the grand sweeping gestures of a mediocre mime artist, ushered Algy into a heaving drawing room.

The room was decorated with some of the most extraordinary specimens Algy had laid eyes on. Women who put the full flam into flamboyant, men who apparently frequented the same dress-makers, and then others who looked as though they'd slipped away from their dreary civil service offices for a meagre bowl of soup. A pair of women standing by the bay window seemed to be staring into a mirror. Similarly proportioned, they wore identical tweed suits, cropped hair and matching monocles. They barely spoke, more intent on looking deep into each other's spare eye than idle chit-chat.

A bald man with an elaborate waxed moustache plucked himself a leather-bound Thomas Mann novel from the bookshelf in the original German; a huddle to Algy's right chuckled knowingly at a risqué Latin joke; a couple played chess with an intricate ivory set made entirely of disrobed kings, queens and pawns; a pair of bespectacled, beaky types discussed the finer points of a Futurist painting by Umberto Boccioni, which hung on the wall, showing ant-like passengers preparing to board a muscular train.

It would have been easy for Algy to feel intimidated by these denizens of the beau monde, but he knew the best course of action. So long as you looked vaguely interested and threw in the occasional "what-what", you'd fare well enough. By and large, people were more than happy to listen to the sounds of their own voices.

"Ahh, a newbie," said a woman in a shimmering turquoise kimono, brushing her feather boa suggestively over Algy's shoulder. "I can tell by the half-open arrangement of your jaws."

"Yes, what-what," said Algy, and then, after some hesitation, "Delighted."

Further pleasantries confirmed that she was Isabella, the hostess's sister. She went on to present Algy with a potted – if slightly potty – history of the Warren. Most of the founders had met some years earlier at a minor university, where they'd formed an unnaturally tight bond. They were a motley collection of writers, artists, musicians, critics, designers, free thinkers, as well as a couple of junior government ministers and a chiropodist. These characters gathered for regular Friday evening soirées, where they drank, smoked and posed copiously, dissecting all the fashionable topics of the day.

"A modern-day salon, if you like daahling," she cooed.

The Warrenites flouted convention, embraced taboo, and delighted in a web of tangled relationships. There were girls who liked boys who liked boys to be girls who did boys like they're girls who did girls like they're boys. And the other way about. Occasionally someone would change sides or "go through a phase," which would put the whole finely balanced eco-system out of kilter. There were devoted twosomes, threesomes and foursomes – Isabella seemed to recall there had even been an eightsome at one stage, though the complicated mechanics of this ménage eluded her. Then, of course, there were the 'floaters', who filled in wherever there happened to be an opening.

The proximity of Warren Street was only one reason for their name, she continued. It also alluded to the underground nature of their activities, and the fact that they were all at it like rabbits. They may not have had the intellectual clout of their illustrious neighbours and arch-rivals the Bloomsbury Group, but when it came to intrigue, decadence and all-round kinkiness, their pedigree, she maintained, was second to none.

Algy mopped his brow with a handkerchief. The room seemed to be getting inordinately hot. And apparently he wasn't the only person who thought so. Someone had placed a table in the centre of the room, on which a languid, reclining woman posed nude, her modesty (not that she possessed much of it) protected only by a plump bunch of grapes and her cascading blonde hair. A petite fellow dressed as Rembrandt, in black breeches and a floppy brimmed hat, stood behind an easel, lustily attacking a canvas with his brush.

It wasn't long before the artist's subject matter had doubled. A lean specimen with a glint in his eye and nothing to be ashamed of positioned himself artfully behind the woman and her grapes. A smiley chap holding a bottle of brandy and a pineapple followed. Then a woman on whose nipples you could hang rain-soaked Barbour jackets. This was the sign. From a trickle, the number of compliant models gradually grew to a stream, transforming the once bare table into a throbbing Bacchanalian tableau, garnished with all manner of suggestive produce.

Algy discreetly peeked at Isabella who was still standing beside him. Her robe was a billowing heap of turquoise beneath her feet, making her look like Aphrodite rising from the surf. She gave him a wink over her shoulder as she slinked across the room to find a sweet spot among the growing scrum of bodies. Much against his better judgement, his character, and everything he'd ever held right and holy, Algy started unbuttoning his rustic suit and, as naked as a young buck on his beloved Warwickshire hills, nervously joined the giggling mêlée.

The Rembrandt impersonator continued to stroke his canvas rhythmically, the only one in the room to retain some semblance of decorum. Or maybe not. As Isabella's hand caressed his goose-bumped thigh, Algy could just make out a pair of black breeches down around his ankles.

"I've got to get myself out of here," thought Algy, nursing his pulsing temples.

He got up slowly, keeping himself slightly hunched, with one hand shielding his manhood and the other strategically positioned over his left nipple. Gingerly, he tip-toed through the sea of comatose souls, desperately searching for his Perkins & Deewbe country-tailored suit.

Algy's cause was hampered by having to avert his eyes from the crusty remnants of countless sleazy misdemeanours, but eventually he caught sight of one of his turn-ups, poking out under a couple of sparked-out, lissom lads. He liberated them with a single desperate pull, and proceeded to collect what he could of the rest of his scrumpled togs. Dressed after a fashion, he quickly made for the door, surprised to see the vendor of last night's *Evening News* asleep in a chair. He was still in his grubby macintosh, but little else, with a small stack of newspapers on his lap. He breathed deeply, emitting a noise that sounded for all the world like "Eeee... nooooo... eeee... noooo".

Algy shut the door behind him and took in some less than fragrant Euston Square air. He set off briskly towards the nearby Tube station, longing for its warmth and anonymity – the comfort of strangers. Only this time, he promised himself, he'd try to keep the levels of comfort in check.

KING'S CROSS

X it

John Simmons

X MARKS THE SPOT. King's Cross yields itself easily to the abbreviation King's X. There's something in it that suggests you have to dig down below the surface to see what you might find. Perhaps that's the explanation for all these construction works. As you come up from deep down inside the Underground (at some point someone dug and discovered a lost tube system) you see men at work, and you hear the thwacks, clunks and whirrs of mechanical equipment. What are they after? Is it just a new parallel universe of the Euston Road or a railway terminal for the trains from France? That's the official story. But there's more to it, there's always more to it.

I've known King's Cross all my life because I was born there in the years after the Second World War. It's forever noisy and forever a site under construction. For the first ten years of my life I looked out from a balcony onto a bombed site. The buildings destroyed in the war became a hole filled with rubble that became a dangerous playground everyday and a venue for a big bonfire on Guy Fawkes' Night. Until eventually a new block of flats rose and became my new view. This was my world.

My world was King's Cross and you left it by going underground. It's a place that exists on a vertical plane in much of my memory. I remember going down into the underground with my dad and brother to the football match at Arsenal – and then we travelled back and up into the daylight or the electric light of an early evening. The sights I remember seeing are mixed with the sounds of clanging, wheezing trains and the smell of smoke and fumes and steam from the railway stations above ground. Walking home to Ossulston Street and passing St Pancras Station on the right – do I really remember its gloomy Gothic magnificence or am I remembering later memories or even earlier Victorian paintings of St Pancras in a landscape? The mind plays tricks. As you grow older it becomes harder to disentangle fact from fiction, memory from imagination. Our memories live in tunnels beneath the surface. Sometimes we bring them up for air. But the exposure to daylight makes them look different.

Dr Cuming, Victorian critic of Underground railways, said: "The forthcoming end of the world would be hastened by the construction of underground railways burrowing into the infernal regions and thereby disturbing the devil." I've never shared this devilish view of the underground railway, I've always seen something romantic in the experience, closer to Ian Marchant's way of looking at railways: "The train you are sitting on is following on the tracks of the Romans' chariots. We are intimately, and at all times, connected with our past, with life, with love, if we could just see it. If we could make the connections."

–O–

From the balcony of my childhood, if I turned my head eastwards, there was an area that might as well have been another bombed site. It was definitely off-limits. There was a high brick wall that you could not see beyond, even from a third-floor balcony. This was railway land: goods yards attached to St Pancras station, the nearer next-door neighbour of King's Cross. In time, too much time, this land would be transformed into the new British Library, a building that like an iceberg conceals most of its enormous bulk beneath the surface.

There's a door in the British Library that takes you down to lower levels. If you can find the door, you'll discover much. Not just about centuries of knowledge through the books gathered there, waiting patiently for a new reader. You'll discover different ways into the past, the present and the future.

The British Library is like a time machine. You can go there to dig down through umpteen layers of the past while sitting comfortably in the present. But in doing so you can think about turning that present and past knowledge into ideas that will mean something in the future. The knowledge you find here can be transformed magically through the power of human memory and imagination.

–O–

Levita House, where I was born, was built in the 1920s as part of slum clearance programmes. Apparently the design was influenced by courtyard layouts borrowed from Vienna, but as a boy I had no thoughts of strudel or schnitzel as I kicked a ball about. Yet now, in that strange foreshortening that you experience when you revisit places in adulthood that once represented your whole world in childhood, there is something reminiscent here of Fritz Lang's *M*. The enormous scale of these buildings in my memory is reduced by reality to tiny echoes of a black and white film set.

Somers Town, as the area is called, was a haven for refugees from the French Revolution. Like most areas of London it has had periods when refugees from different communities have colonised it. Today people from Somalia and Bangladesh are dominant, and they have their community centres. Tomorrow refugees from another part of the world. At the age of twelve I felt the pain of dislocation. Forty or more years ago my uprooting involved a journey of three miles rather than three thousand, from one street in the city to another, rather than from one continent to another. But I still remember the tears I cried when we were about to leave, I remember the white bedsheet I pulled over my eyes in the dark, I remember the sound of the trains pulling out of the station that still haunts me down the years.

It's a strange experience going back. I come up from underground through the building works that is King's Cross Tube station this winter in 2005. I head north, stopping to see some of the new station being built, then looping round with the gasholder on the near horizon. Over there were streets that until just the other day were used for filming scenes of Victorian life. Where will the film industry go for its period shots when the twenty-first century asserts itself fully here? The road bends round to Camley Street.

–O–

Camley Street Natural Park is a surprise to the passing visitor, although it would be a surprising visitor who just happened to be passing. Seek it out. Locked between roads, canal and railway lines, with a gasholder looming in the sky, it's a haven for wildlife. You walk in through gates that say "No Dogs" and tramp up and down paths ("Don't leave the paths and trample our fragile ecosystem"). You look for animals and you see them mentioned on the notices – "water for frogs, foxes" but expect the real ones to be wearing earmuffs. The clanging of the construction sites, the roar of the traffic; urban cacophony is a constant background. But then underneath it all you hear a bird singing, and the water rushing through the canal lock. Your ears learn to filter out the unwanted noises and concentrate just on those sounds that are right for a wildlife park. But then the Midland mainline screeches by across the railway bridge just 50 yards away.

You exit passing by a plastic kitchen basin that says: "Even a pond this small can attract amphibians, insects, birds and foxes."

–O–

Just across the road, past the bridge, is St Pancras churchyard. Thomas Godwin is buried here, and it's the Soane family spot too. Godwin's wife, Mary Wollstonecraft, died 1797, lies here too. St Pancras, it seems, heard a message about women's rights long before my mum came along.

In the church graveyard there's a different kind of quiet. It turns out to be no surprise that the handsome Gothic building is the Coroner's Court. It's convenient after all. *Erected 1886.* A tablet set in the wall commemorates the work of the Sanitary Committee that placed it here, among the medieval bones of the churchyard. This setting, with the hospital for tropical diseases next door, reveals the meaning of *memento mori*. Remember: everything passes. In King's Cross, you can see the layers of passing, as long as you look for them.

Just there is the Hardy Tree, an ash tree that has grown up as if its shoulders have risen to push aside headstones ready for the resurrection. In 1865, Thomas Hardy (yes that one) studied architecture in London under a Covent Garden architect, Arthur Blomfield. Hardy was given the task of overseeing the exhumation of remains and dismantling of tombs to make way for the railway line. No wonder he got depressed "because we are too menny."

St Pancras Old Church, one of Europe's most ancient sites of Christian worship, dates to the early fourth century. More than a millennium later it became the barracks for Cromwell's men in the Civil War. Anticipating this event, its treasures were buried for safekeeping and then lost. They weren't rediscovered until restoration in the nineteenth century. But restoration after restoration has left little visible of the ancient original. Now it's an elegant Victorian church, but the phantoms remain of its former lives.

Across the road, Goldington Crescent is elegant and I used to get off the trolley bus here on my way home from school. Asked by one of my new schoolfriends where I was heading, I once said "Golders Green" by mistake – it was where most of my school's pupils came from. There's still a big gap in affluence between the two places although the houses around the corner at the northern end of Ossulston Street give the impression of waiting to be discovered by property developers who will spruce them up and double the prices.

–O–

Further down the street, past the school and the community centres, you come to Levita House. It's a grey, solid estate that once was famously progressive, named after Cecil Levita who had been chairman of the London County Council. The naming itself is a way of honouring the past. The stone on the side of the building proclaims that His Majesty's Minister for Health, Neville Chamberlain, opened Levita House in 1928. It was a short step from there to naïve meetings with Herr Hitler a decade later, waving the piece of paper that has come to symbolise the futility of raised hopes.

Now the lights have been going out in Levita House. It's a solid monument to the hopes of an earlier generation of social reformers. With a little investment these flats would be sold off to the wealthy, so there's part of me that's grateful that today's near dereliction is almost a guarantee of preservation for a little longer of ungentrified life.

There's the balcony, third floor up, where our flat was and where I was born. Shall I go up? No, too many ghosts. And anyway the security gates mean that you cannot get in unless you know a current resident. "NO BALL GAMES" it says. How would I have survived? Playing with a ball, whether for football or cricket, was the central activity of my childhood – the rest of my life revolved around it.

The sight of those balconies up there releases the memories of Emmy Beerman, rolling in drunkenly singing at midnight, ready next day to make more funeral wreaths. Dolly Jessup, Biddy Beevor, Little Edie, my mum's friends. I can't quite face these memories, because I'm too aware that they are now fading into shadows. If I try hard to call them back, am I simply exercising my imagination rather than my memory? But is there that much of a difference?

–O–

I cut through into Chalton Street. In my memory it is long and wide, but it's now diminished by the shrinking process of growing older. Fred Field's Hardware Shop has become a Filipino Centre. The Coop has turned into a Costcutter. The Coffee House, no Starbucks this, but a pub that for me will always be the off-licence where I was sent on errands to buy a Guinness as a nightcap for my mother. The fish and chip shop where I used to take the week's newspapers to exchange for a couple of coppers or a bag of chips has been boarded up. The Vic, my mum and dad's old pub of choice, has become an oriental restaurant. The sweet shop is an anonymous computer business. The pub on the corner, once the Rising Sun, now the Rocket in some kind of nod to railway tradition, is full of fruit machines. It was on the doorstep of this pub in 1922 that my mother-in-law came into the world. Her dad was taking her mum to hospital on the back of a milk float, when nature decided that horse travel was not fast enough, and out popped Liz Wheatley. If her newborn eyes saw anything of her surroundings, they saw Chalton Street, but a different one from the one that I grew up in or that stands there now.

Just there too she might have seen a wide gathering place, in the space between Chalton Street and Ossulston Street that's now a theatre. I remember that space as being like Trafalgar Square, but I realise now that it was no more than a courtyard. Here my mum took me to hear angry speeches urging tenants to join the rent strike. Across the road Labour councillors hoisted the red flag above St Pancras Town Hall in an act that shocked the establishment. There was a taste of rebellion in the air and Jessie Simmons was one of the rebels, one of a line of remarkable women from King's Cross, stretching back to Boadicea who legend says was buried here, down below the pavements we now stand on. But there is no cross to mark her place in history.

King's Cross takes its name from a statue of King George IV that once stood here. The cross also means that this place is an intersection, a place for coming together from many different directions, then striking off again to any point of the cross that is a compass. If you head south, over the barrier of the Euston Road, you find yourself in a quiet, secluded area where people live in elegant houses around squares and gardens. It's a lovely village-like part of London and well worth exploring. But my space is confined, I'm heading north and a little west because that's where I was born. And, for me, until the age of about 12, this was my world.

In the meantime, just observe that the highest points of both St Pancras and King's Cross stations are compasses or weather vanes marked (how else?) NESW. Go west, young man, or you could try north, east or south too. The area invites you to look beyond its immediate locations.

There are worlds to discover in London. You can start at King's Cross. Just go through the door marked X.

ABOUT THE WRITERS

Simon Armitage *King's Cross*
Simon Armitage has published nine collections of poetry and two novels. He is also a playwright and broadcaster, and has written extensively for film, television and radio.

Jayne Workman *Farringdon*
Jayne Workman is a writer at brand and design consultancy Elmwood. Other passions include travel in India, Iyengar's tree posture, horse-riding and trying to speak Spanish.

Mike Reed *Barbican*
Mike Reed has been writing stories since he could write, and copywriting since 1993. Now freelance, he works mainly in the design field. His last published fiction was in 1989.

Elise Valmorbida *Moorgate*
Elise Valmorbida grew up Italian in Australia, but fell in love with London. She is a designer and writer. Her first published novel was *Matilde Waltzing*.

Tom Lynham *Liverpool Street*
Tom Lynham tried to change the world by inventing the Televisor and designing the Unfinished Table, but now he does it by writing stories.

Rishi Dastidar *Aldgate*
Rishi Dastidar works for customer-experience consultancy Seren in London. In his free time, he woos glamorous and inappropriate women – sometimes successfully – with words and pictures.

Karen McCarthy *Mark Lane*
Karen McCarthy was born in Belsize Park. She left NW3 for NW6 and now lives down in SW2. Her favourite tube line is still the Bakerloo.

Acknowledgement Thanks to the staff at Tower Hill, particularly Sue Jackman and Darren Houghton, and also to Alec Taylor, a Freeman of the City of London whom I accosted on India Street. We didn't talk for long, but his love for the City and willingness to share its history was heartening.

Anelia Schutte *Tower Hill*
Anelia Schutte writes copy for a living and bad poetry for fun. She lives in London but comes from Knysna, where there are no ravens, just elephants.

Acknowledgement With thanks to Derrick Coyle, Ravenmaster, for his kindness.

Tim Segaller *River Link*
Tim Segaller had an averagely unaverage childhood. Grew up, nearly. Read dead languages for ages, then forgot them – giving his brain space to write in the English language.

Neil Taylor *Monument*
Neil Taylor is a Belle and Sebastian fan, linguistics bore, born-again Doctor Who devotee, Southwark cyclist, Blackburn supporter and writer and trainer at The Writer.

Dan Germain *Cannon Street*
Dan Germain is tall, tired and sometimes has a beard. He played the violin for a bit when he was eight and his favourite colour is maths.

Simon Jones *Mansion House*
A creative and business writer, Simon Jones recently co-founded Ink Copywriters to help companies find their unique voice and use words more effectively.

Acknowledgement Christian, thanks for all your help along the way.

Nick Asbury *Blackfriars*
Nick Asbury writes for design companies and occasionally about them. He is the co-author of *Alas! Smith & Milton: How not to run a design company.*

Tim Rich *Temple*
Tim Rich is a London-based writer and editor. He is a founder of 26 and co-edited the book *26 Letters: Illuminating the alphabet.*

Acknowledgement Thanks to Paul Davis and William Bennett.

Rob Williams *Embankment*
Rob Williams is a Brummie who daydreams about spending more time wandering round public spaces like his subject and writing with the integrity of Tony Parker.

Tim Coates *Westminster*
Tim Coates is a Bloomsbury author praised for his book about Patsy Cornwallis-West and his edited collections from contemporary documents about Henry VIII and Florence Nightingale.

David May *St James's Park*

David May is the BBC's head of strategic communications. He has co-authored two books, co-edited *Time Out*, news-edited the *Sunday Times* and produced documentaries for Channel Four.

Acknowledgements I am indebted to Helen Kent of the Transport for London Library for providing invaluable source material; Liz O'Sullivan of Platform Art for her insight into public art; David Leboff for being such a willing tour guide; Beth Mercer for providing archive documents; Mo Ibrahim, St James's Park supervisor, for his knowledge of the station; and Obrenka Milošević for editorial support.

Dan Radley *Victoria*

Dan Radley travelled by Underground to school in Victoria in the 1970s. His world revolved around football, music, girls and regurgitating useless information. Worryingly, it still does.

Acknowledgement Thanks to Amanda Radley for keeping me buoyant. To Carole and Chris Radley, my amazing archivists. To the Driver family for confirming the ghastly details. To everyone at Start for being so enthusiastic about 26. To Gideon Sams for writing *The Punk*. To all those who recognise themselves in the essay; I hope you're not offended and life is treating you well.

Will Awdry *Sloane Square*

Will Awdry: Working life: packing up sales patter into advertisements. Home life: packing up after two small children. In between: unpacking whimsical fantasies about scribbling a whole book.

Martin Gorst *South Kensington*

Martin Gorst is a freelance television writer and director specialising in science documentaries. He is the author of *Aeons: The search for the beginning of time*.

Gordon Kerr *Gloucester Road*

Freelance consultant, writer, editor and poet, currently editing a *Poetry Writers' & Artists' Yearbook* for publication, autumn 2006 and hiding from harsh reality in deepest Hampshire.

Sarah McCartney *High Street Kensington*

Sarah McCartney was accidentally born in Saltburn by the Sea instead of Italy. When not writing she teaches yoga, sips espresso and knits her own woollies.

Lisa Desforges *Notting Hill Gate*

Lisa Desforges is head of words at a design consultancy called Pearlfisher, where she encourages colleagues and clients to use very big pictures and very little copy.

Laura Forman *Bayswater*
Now: copywriter and copy manager, John Lewis
Before: senior writer, Interbrand
Before that: natural sciences, Cambridge
Always: poetry, singing, cooking, reading, fun things

Ian Marchant *Paddington*
Ian Marchant's six books include *Parallel Lines*, a sort of history of Britain's railways. For candid photographs of the author, visit *www.ianmarchant.com.*

David Varela *Edgware Road*
David Varela writes short films, short stories, long poems, and things for radio and theatre, which sometimes win awards. He also helps companies find their voice.

Acknowledgement Thanks go to Simon Connor, Stephen Cross, Anna Cumming and Amin Qulatein for their encouragement. And thank you, Anelia, for help beyond words.

Steve Mullins *Control Room*
Steve Mullins works with words and images. And plays with the same.

Acknowledgement Simon Flatau and Sue Butcher of London Underground.

Stuart Delves *Baker Street*
Stuart Delves is co-founder of Henzteeth, Edinburgh. Writes for cobalt-blue-chip clients then heads for the hills (literally) to be with artist wife and two highly entertaining children.

Richard Owsley *Great Portland Street*
Richard Owsley was born in 1957 and grew up in north London suburbia. He now lives in Bristol with his wife and three children.

Acknowledgment I'd like to thank my colleagues at Writers, and my wife's book-club members, for providing invaluable comments on my working drafts.

Jim Davies *Euston Square*
Jim Davies writes for and about the design industry. He has a monthly column in *Design Week*, and reads more P. G. Wodehouse than he ought to.

John Simmons *King's Cross*
John Simmons: writer-in-chief at The Writer, founder director of 26, editor of *Great brand stories*, and author of books including *My sister's a barista* and *Dark angels*.

ACKNOWLEDGEMENTS

This book grew out of a project for the London Design Festival that also involved London Underground and the London College of Communications. Other aspects of the creative collaboration included posters, an exhibition and a website. Although these are not directly part of this book, they all contributed to the content here in some way. So although we have tried to name as many people as possible, we are unable to name everyone simply because there have been so many participants. We apologise to any we have missed.

Our thanks first of all to Lynne Dobney and the London Design Festival. Lynne invited 26's participation and we were delighted to respond. Helen Horton Smith, William Knight and John Sorrell have been good supporters of 26 and the Circle Line project.

At the London College of Communications, Sarah Temple has been creative, determined and a pleasure to work with. She brought her colleagues on board, including the Dean, Mike Bradshaw, and she was our main contact with students and staff. She was ably assisted by Jenny Clarke.

Liz O'Sullivan, head of Platform for Art at London Underground is a wonder. She has enough energy to power the Tube system but she does it with charm and intellect too. She was brilliantly supported by Sara-Ellen Williams. This book and the whole Circle Line project owe them an enormous debt.

The general manager of the Circle Line, Peter Tollington, ensured that this project happened with the support of London Underground staff. Volunteers at each of the stations helped out writers with research, queries and sometimes ideas. We're particularly grateful to the following people from London Underground who helped with the preparation of this book and the related exhibition: Peter Harris (Aldgate), Oladapo Akinola and Trevor Baker (Baker Street), Paul Ibbott (Barbican), Brian Haughian (Bayswater), Norman Harford (Blackfriars), Tony Wallington (Cannon Street), Simon Flatau (Control Room), Robert Fletcher-Jones, Walter Maidment and Mags Nash (Edgware Road), Karmanie Kasturiratne and Brian Liddle (Embankment), Barry Hensey (Euston Square), Paul Ibbott (Farringdon), David Hickey and Chris Turner (Gloucester Road), Dapo Akinola and Eric Reeve (Great Portland Street), Lew Macintosh and staff (High Street Kensington), Ken Leach

(King's Cross St Pancras), Jane Reade (Liverpool Street), Stephen Markey, Brian Richards and Chris Shelton (Mansion House), Phil Huggett, Mickey James and Martin Walker (Monument), Tom O'Riordan and Davis Odelli (Moorgate), Vick Keeler and Marcus Storey (Notting Hill), Robert Fletcher-Jones (Paddington), Kevin Keegan and Pat Webb (Sloane Square), Andrew Gaskin (South Kensington), Mo Ibrahim (St James's Park), Karmanie Kasturiratne (Temple), Darren Houghton and Jeff Withaj (Tower Hill), Simon White (Victoria), Maria Shake (Westminster), Mike Baxter, Sue Butcher, Charlotte Fynn, Dave Hembury, Dave Hirst, Susan Jackman, Helen Kent, David Leboff, Tony O'Donnell, Nick Orange, Peter Sanders, Lisa Sparrow and Stevyn Walder (group station managers), Mark Charrington, Katie Day, Anya Oliver and Louise Wilshaw (Platform for Art) and the unknown train driver.

Arts & Business have provided funding that helped the Circle Line project to happen. We're particularly grateful to Mark Da Vanzo for his support and advice.

Our publishers Cyan have shown belief and commitment in this book. We're very grateful to Martin Liu, Pom Somkabcharti and Linette Tye for all their hard work and care. Jessie Simmons took the black and white photographs to accompany each of the chapters. Rob Andrews and David Carroll of R&D&Co, also members of 26, have designed the book beautifully – and with Gilmar Wendt they gave time and expertise to the LCC students.

Finally we have to thank our colleagues in 26. When we formed 26 in 2003 we didn't imagine we would be involved in projects like this. It has happened as quickly as it has because of the enthusiasm of so many 26 members, not only the ones who have contributed to this book.

www.26.org.uk

London Underground

UNIVERSITY OF THE ARTS LONDON **LONDON COLLEGE OF COMMUNICATION** CAMBERWELL COLLEGE OF ARTS CENTRAL SAINT MARTINS COLLEGE OF ART AND DESIGN CHELSEA COLLEGE OF ART AND DESIGN LONDON COLLEGE OF FASHION

THE LONDON DESIGN FESTIVAL 2005

Arts & Business *New Partners*

platform
art

26